If HISTORY HAS
TAUGHT US ANYTHING

❦

Farhat Nasreen is a Professor of History at Jamia Millia Islamia, New Delhi. Her work *Kashful Baghaavat Gorakhpur* presents an extremely rare eyewitness account of the Revolt of 1857. She has authored several monographs and articles on historical themes.

If HISTORY HAS TAUGHT US ANYTHING

Farhat Nasreen

Published by
Rupa Publications India Pvt. Ltd 2019
7/16, Ansari Road, Daryaganj
New Delhi 110002

Sales Centres:
Allahabad Bengaluru Chennai
Hyderabad Jaipur Kathmandu
Kolkata Mumbai

Copyright © Farhat Nasreen 2019

The views and opinions expressed in this book are the author's own and the facts are as reported by her which have been verified to the extent possible, and the publishers are not in any way liable for the same.

All rights reserved.
No part of this publication may be reproduced, transmitted, or stored in a retrieval system, in any form or by any means, electronic, mechanical, photocopying, recording or otherwise, without the prior permission of the publisher.

ISBN: 978-93-5333-478-9

First impression 2019

10 9 8 7 6 5 4 3 2 1

Printed at Nutech Print Services, Faridabad

The moral right of the author has been asserted.

This book is sold subject to the condition that it shall not, by way of trade or otherwise, be lent, resold, hired out, or otherwise circulated, without the publisher's prior consent, in any form of binding or cover other than that in which it is published.

Contents

Foreword / vii

Introduction: Swearing by the Passage of Time / ix

1. Valorous Vikram and His Brothers / 1
2. A Persian Epic and a Betrayal of Epic Proportions / 14
3. From Qutbuddin to Qutbuddin and the Bloodlust in Between / 35
4. Humanness and Baadshah Humayun / 101
5. Shielding the Show: Sher Shah— A Manager Par Excellence / 130
6. The Last Word: An Equilibrial Mantra, Sulh-i kul / 147

Conclusion: Looking Back, and the Omnipresent Past / 185

Bibliography / 195

Index / 199

Foreword

I am happy that Professor Farhat Nasreen has given us a work that is designed to illustrate what lessons one can draw from History. After all, pursuit of History is justified only if it can affect our practice; it is like the memory of one's own past experiences that guides an individual in his or her ordinary conduct. For history, like memory, to serve best, the primary requirement is that it should be accurate—not only in facts but also in its assessments of those facts.

This, often, given the limitations of our sources, places a heavy demand on the historians, and it is no wonder that historians so often differ among themselves—less over facts, perhaps, than over assessments. Professor Nasreen wisely takes her information from various sources by largely letting them speak for themselves, and leaves us to draw lessons ourselves.

So let us now read and form our own judgements and draw from the narratives of the past that she sets out.

Irfan Habib

Introduction

Swearing by the Passage of Time

If people injure thee grieve not
Because neither rest nor grief come from the people
Be aware that the contrasts of friend and foe are from God
Because the hearts of both are in his keeping
Although the arrow is shot from the bow
Wise men look at the archer.

—SAADI SHIRAZI: *The Golestan*[1]

Time is a free-flowing highway. The unbreakable and timeless chain of its byways can perhaps be attributed to the strength with which it tethers present to the past.

When historians speak of causation they imply that all occurrences are correlated by cause and effect. However, it is not always easy to spot the interconnecting chain of event-impact-event or situation-response-situation. When a turnout is under process the links are unclear. On the other

---

[1] Saadi Shirazi, *The Golestan*, Richard Francis Burton (translation), Iran Chamber Society, p. 44.

hand, after a long time lapse they are buried under layers of eventualities. No wonder then, that more complex than collecting factual data is establishing its relationship with cause and effect. Therefore, a crucial tool for reconstructing the chain is contemporaneous documentation. In this context, the works of contemporary historians are like time machines. Free of duration-triggered amnesia and greased with objectivity, they can bring the dead back to life.

Deductions of patterns of historical repetition indicate that while subjective templates like name, place and time change, the structural construct of situations remains mostly unaltered. To navigate humans through a rerun of situations, truism emerges like a guide. Time-tested choices are passed into theory as ethics and value systems. No wonder it became axiomatic that good begets good.

Historians, as time travellers, encounter and relive extremely potent events. They call on men who have overcome death and who inspire them like muses. In ancient Greek religion, the muses were nine sister goddesses—the daughters of Zeus and Mnemosyne, the goddess of memory. Thus the keepers of time provide elixir to memories. Historicism is inescapable, in the sense that all humans have some story to tell and, ultimately, they themselves become stories. Thus there are boundless stories in the annals of time. Most of these remain untold. Out of those told, a few are retold. Their sporadic narration continues even at the risk of causing déjà vu and evoking the same love or hate that they might have generated in the past. These myths are valuable for their ability to flip perspectives.

Introduction: Swearing by the Passage of Time • xi

Humans face enormous choices, locked up in challenges. Their decisions unlock opportunities. If we suppose that history repeats itself, then sifting through the most advantageous choices made in the past could unearth clues for better choices in the future. The past, in a way, tips off the present. Even after making concessions to confidence and the trickster called fate, a lot can still be attributed to human thought and action. A recapitulation of the past may not help us solve all the puzzles of life in the first go, but it at least prepares us to fail better. Indeed, every bygone event has left something for the present.

This historiated text rests on a presumption of equilibrium between the statics and dynamics of the past and the present. Therefore, it uses history as a blueprint for reading human minds. The characters of the stories presented here were implicated in the power relations of their times. Therefore, using current standards to judge, criticize or mythologize them would be unfair. Likewise, deconstructing time frames and labelling them as good or bad can be tricky. It is indeed extraordinary that religions foretold the detrimental effect of 'time' on the times and so, predictably, 'good old times' became a proverb. Human existence is a very fragile construct in ways beyond the physical here and now. As we move on in life, what we leave behind becomes irretrievable—and it might have been just fine that way, had it not been for our power to remember, rue and regret. In fact, the various uses that memory is put to have become a threat to human peace. In this context, notwithstanding the importance of experimentation, experience—which itself is based on previous experiments—becomes a kind of users' manual. At an individual level, time overtakes life. However, in the context of generational cycles and the individuals within them, History, in all its dynamism, continues to accompany time. A self-fashioning form of art, it knows no dead-time or dead-end.

II

This text presents an assortment of events where History is the narratologist, the narrator and the narratee. Motivated by an enthusiastic quest to understand oneself in context of the known immediate and the unknown past and future, this book focuses on facts beyond data. Historical texts are escorts in this search because they are equipped to guide seekers. Different students take away different lessons from the same lecture. This narrative seeks smartly ethical pathways for thoughts and actions. The first chapter narrates the story of Vikramjeet/Vikramaditya, the great monarch of ancient India, drawn from the *Singhasan Battisi* or the *Namah-e Khirad Afza* (as the Persian translation was called). However, the spotlight here is shared by his two brothers, Sankh and Bharatari, who present the extremes of ambition and renunciation. The second account is of the shameful betrayal of Firdausi, the author of the epic *Shahnama* by his patron, the rich and powerful Sultan Mahmud of Ghazni. Mahmud defaulted on the amount he had promised to pay the poet. Though he thought that he could get away with it, he didn't. The third section deals with one of the most vibrant periods of Indian history, the Sultanate. This is when extensive integration of lands began, armies were better organized, governance became more centralized and fashionably opulent court etiquettes emerged. Even though the Divine Right Theory of Kingship and letters of recognition from the Khalifa of Baghdad were used as tools for political legitimization, this phase was marked by shockingly violent usurpations. Interestingly, since the administration was quite personality-centric, every Sultan marked it with the design he preferred. Policies, court culture and even courtiers changed when a new usurper emerged as the sultan. This chapter elaborates that while ambition's horrifying roller coaster crushed many, its drivers also couldn't escape being squashed by the hammer of natural justice. The following chapter has anecdotes relating the administrative and managerial skills of the quick-witted Afghan ruler of India, Sher Shah Suri. Despite his humble beginnings, Sher Shah was able to oust Humayun, who had a head start on him by virtue of being Babur's son and heir. Suri not only outmaneuvered his rivals, but in the short span of his reign, made such valuable policies of governance that they formed guidelines for none other than the greatest of the Mughals, Akbar.

The following section has to do with Humayun, probably the most modest of the Mughal emperors and my personal favourite. He was a giver surrounded by takers and due to simple-mindedness he looked for the right answers at the wrong places. If one evaluates his political and military skills, he would be a mediocre, but his success as a humanitarian is what we celebrate. The last part has to do with Sulh-i kul: Absolute Peace/Universal Peace. The idea was the brainchild of Akbar, initially prompted by his tutor Mir Abdul Latif and later nourished by his think tank of liberals like Shaikh Mubarak and his brilliant sons Faizi and Abul Fazl, the author of *Akbarnama*. An aura of mysticism, merriment and magic exudes from this notion of peace, and Akbar made this invisible emanation visible by a conscious policy of non-judgemental acceptance. The reason for this being the last section is that in my interactions with stalwart historians like Satish Chandra, Harbans Mukhia, D.N. Jha, Iqtidar Husain Siddiqui and Shireen Moosvi, I found that the common denominator in their opinions is the importance of humanism. Their valuable inputs are included in the concluding section. Thus Absolute Peace/Universal Peace emerges as the last word.

The immobility of the words resting in books is deceptive, because they actually move in human minds. The thoughts that they generate motivate actions, and actions make or unmake many things—like progress and relationships. In this sense, words energize men and men, in turn, beautify them. Words have a life of their own and it is a reasonably long one; far beyond that of their speakers or writers. Books of History don't only bequeath legends to posterity; they act as very compelling emotion intensifiers. It is not just about saying or writing something historical; it is about an unspoken relationship between men and their past. The historian, as a driving force, negotiates variables of experiences to create a magical space. In this space various elements cooperate with each other to create a society—a collective memory—a way of thinking. Self images are made and unmade by stories of bygone days. Just as individuals enjoy recollecting their childhood, societies relish their histories. In fact, because of the remarkable expertise of History in intensifying emotions, it has always been used by the powers that be to generate sentiments in the masses. It is used to steer upheavals or design settlements. When the cumulative effect of the passions of sorrow or elation, love or hate goes out of hand, it becomes a weapon which needs to be handled with extreme caution. For individuals, history has a mystical charm which helps one in connecting with the self and the cosmos at the very same time. As a sole witness to irretrievable times, its importance cannot be overstated; however, its softly floating whispers often go unnoticed in the maddening preoccupations of the immediately urgent. This collection of anecdotes contends that the past is mysterious and yet unambiguous, and hopes that readers would be drawn into its mystic sorcery in such a way that they would see beyond names, dates and data—because what stands veiled behind them is rather enchanting.

Historians, like advocates, can argue a case for opposing sides. They can plead for both peace and war. It is a choice that they make all the time. However, History itself teaches that all such fragments of the past, which can hurt people like broken glass does, should be handled with care. It is crucial to strike a balance between remembering and forgetting; between holding on and letting go.

Chapter I

Valorous Vikram and His Brothers

Not one amongst the philosophers of Greece or Rome could produce honey from a thorn... A mirror can be freed of stain but it cannot be made from stone... O irresolute one! Be tranquil, for grass grows not on revolving stones.

—Saadi Shirazi, *The Bustan*[1]

Timeline: Vikram Samvat is a calendar era starting from 57 BCE. This calendar uses lunar months and the solar sidereal year.[2]

---

[1] Sadi Shirazi, *Bustan*, cf. *The Bustan of Sadi*, A. Hart Edwards, Kitab Bhavan, New Delhi, 2000, pp. 74 and 77.

[2] D.C. Sircar opines that this era came to be known as Vikram Samvat following the reign of the Gupta monarch Chandragupta II who was chosen to rule among the many sons of Samudragupta and his reign has been dated between 375/6 and 413/4 CE. Upinder Singh agrees with the dating of the rule of Chandragupta II and mentions that he was adorned with epithets such as 'Parama-Bhagavata' and 'Vikramaditya' to highlight his political invincibility and establish his affiliation to the Vaishnava cult. During his rule the Gupta Empire reached the peak of its territorial expansion. However, though Ashvini Agrawal

Backdrop: This section has two narratives derived from the *Singhasan Battisi*.[3] They are related to the life and times of the legendary king Virkramjeet/Vikramaditya who, according to this text, is the founder of the Vikram Samvat, a calendar era starting from 57 BCE. It is believed that Vikramjeet had a magnificent throne which was gifted to him by Bahubal, a powerful ruler. Studded with priceless gems, the seat of the throne was supported by statues of thirty-two apsaras (nymphs), eight statues on each of its four sides, holding lotuses in their hands. They were crafted in moulds laced with elixir and seemed miraculously alive. Their motivated lips and eyes negated their static figures. The supernatural qualities of the throne supposedly exemplified the power and piety of its possessor. However, having a certain level of prelapsarian greatness was a prerequisite for owning it.

Many years after Vikram's demise, Raja Bhoj, the king of Ujjain, accidentally discovered the throne buried under a mound. It was reported to him that a poor farmer who grew cucumbers used to display exceptional wisdom and egalitarianism whenever he sat on a particular mound. This feat had gained such popularity that crowds of people gathered to present their cases and see him deliver exemplary justice. Bhoj had heard legends of Vikramjeet's throne and its special powers. Thus he had the mysterious

---

agrees with D.C. Sircar, he further elaborates that this era, staring from 57 BCE was already in existence, known as kṛta, the era of the Malava tribe or as simply Samvat.
[3]*Singhasan Battisi*, Lalluji Lal Kabi (translation from Sanskrit to Hindi), Syed Abdoollah (revised and corrected with copious notes), W.H. Allen &Co, London, 1869.

site excavated and the throne was recovered. It was quickly restored to its former magnificence with the help of jewelsmiths and craftsmen. An auspicious day and time was selected for the king to be formally seated on it. As a prelude to the proposed ceremony, land grants were given to priests, salaries of the armymen were raised, the poor were fed and clothed with unprecedented generosity and friends and family engaged in ostentatious merriment. On the appointed day and hour the king approached the throne and as his loyal nobility and enthusiastic subjects watched, the thirty-two statues came alive and scoffed at his audacious intention. Bhoj was dismayed at their hostile mockery. He asked them to explain themselves. In response, each one of them narrated an anecdote expressing Vikramjeet's greatness.[4] They impressed upon Bhoj that only someone as great as Vikramjeet deserved to be seated on it. Although by and large caste stereotypes are prevalent throughout the *Singhasan Battisi,* it does not shy from highlighting intra-caste tensions.

The Mughal emperor Akbar was particularly fond of the *Singhasan Battisi* and had it translated into Persian, with the title *Namah-e Khirad Afza* (*The Book of Mental Recreation/ The Enhancer of Wisdom*). Abdul Qadir Badaoni, who headed the team of translators, compared it with the classic *Tuti Namah*. He reports that Akbar's queen Salima Sultan Begum had also read the *Khirad Afza*. It so happened that Akbar's copy of the book disappeared from the royal library and a vexed Akbar sent messengers to Badaoni with

---

[4] Ibid., pp. 5–9.

orders to demand the book from him whether he liked it or not. As a punishment for the lost copy, his Madad-e Maash payment was stopped and the fellow received no salary. He further reports that Rai Purushottam was rewarded by Akbar for writing a commentary on the same and was promoted to the post of Bakshi.[5] In 1866, this text was chosen by the British Civil Service Commission as a text book for aspirants of the Indian Civil Service.

The following narratives are derived from the discourse between two statues named Ratanmanjari and Chitrarekha. These are about Vikram and his brothers. His elder brother Sankh displays qualities of greed and deceit while Bhartari, the younger one, renounces the world to become an ascetic.

◆

Sankh's Sorcery and Bahubal's Bounty

Gandharvasen, the king of Ambavati, had four wives belonging to the four classical varnas (castes)—Brahmin, Kshatriya, Vaishya and Shudra. The Brahmin wife bore him one son named Birhanjeet. He became such an astute scholar of astronomy that he could predict even births and deaths with reasonable accuracy. The Kshatriya queen bore three sons named Sankh, Vikram and Bhartari. Their bravery earned them the title of 'Kalpavriksha'; the

---

[5]Abdul Qadir Badaoni, *Muntakhab-ut Tawarikh*, Vol.II, G.S.A. Ranking (translation), Saeed International, New Delhi, 1990, pp. 265, 274, 389 and 426.

undying tree. The Vaishya queen's son Chandra was a rich merchant famous for his generosity and kindness. Lastly, Dhanvantra, born of the Shudra queen, was a great medical practitioner.[6] Sankh, Vikram's elder brother, was eventually crowned the king. However, the priests predicted that he would be assassinated and ultimately Vikram would rule. In view of his brother's ascetic tendencies and his own perceived invincibility, Sankh jeered at the prediction of the priests. One day he was apprised by intelligence agents that Vikram, who had become a yogi, was meditating and praying in the jungles on the outskirts of his kingdom. He went there in hiding and watched Vikram from a distance. His brother's calmness and his own anxiety enraged him and maddened by rage, he urinated on the icon that Vikram was worshipping. The outraged Brahmins reprimanded him but their admonitions fell on deaf ears. Murmurs flew that the king's downfall was near, because he had drowned in arrogance.

Sankh conspired to use black magic to put down his brother, whom he presumed to be his enemy. Seven spellbinding lines were drawn with charmed coal at the entrance of a room. Anyone who stepped over them was supposed to go insane. Secondly, a magicked cucumber and knife were procured. Their sorcerous power would slit the throat of the man who cut the cucumber. He was to invite Vikram into this trap. The Kshatriyas condemned Sankh's plan because it entailed killing someone treacherously and not in fair combat. Luckily, Vikram himself had reasonable

---
[6]Ibid., p. 11.

knowledge of such crafts and he sensed the enchantment. Skipping the lines at the entrance, he severed Sankh's head instead of slicing the cucumber. When he stepped out of that room with blood smeared on his forehead, it became known that Ambavati had a new king.[7]

Although Vikram had not intended to kill his brother, it is the latter's insecurities that paved the way for such a showdown, which only one of them could have survived.

Hunting was a prevalent sport for the royals. They were usually accompanied by a train of soldiers, hounds, falcons, bird catchers and other facilitators. On one such expedition a deer chase drew Vikram deep into the jungles. As the frenzied hunt speeded up, the entourage was lost and the king found himself amidst a green sea of trees that quickly turned black as the sun went down. He climbed a tree to figure out a way. In the distance he saw a dance of reassuring lights, illuminating a nearby town. In a fit of spontaneous inspiration, he resolved to integrate that enthralling place into his kingdom.

Lutbaran, a minister of that realm, was an accomplished sorcerer. Disguised as a crow, he was flying past at that very moment. Agitated by the king's intentions, he defecated on him. The next morning, a directive was issued to capture all the crows of the jungle. The bird catchers made the most of this strange order and within no time, all the crows were entrapped. If the audacious one that had befouled the king did not confess, he would take all of their lives. Vikram had sensed some wizardry, and the crows of course knew that

---

[7]Ibid., pp. 12–15.

the culprit was the sorcerer Lutbaran, minister of the king Bahubal. When they disclosed this to Vikram, he freed two of the crows to persuade Lutbaran to surrender, while the others were held as collateral. On hearing of their plight, Lutbaran immediately presented himself. Vikram received him with humility and all the birds were freed.

The minister informed the king that it was Bahubal's kingdom that had caught King Vikram's attention. He revealed to the king that before becoming an independent monarch, Vikram's father Gandharva Sen had served as an officer of Bahubal. Therefore, ideally, Vikram should seek formal recognition of independence from his father's benefactor, King Bahubal, and secure his blessings. The wise Brahmin's advice easily prevailed upon the king because he was very scrupulous in matters of propriety. Finally, on an auspicious day and time, Vikram proceeded to meet King Bahubal. On hearing of his arrival, Bahubal made the most ostentatious arrangements for the comfortable stay of his royal guest. Vikram was overwhelmed by his host's humility and munificence.

After a few days, he told Lutbaran that he wanted to return home. The minister informed him that as per convention, he would require the host's permission, and given Bahubal's unprecedented largesse he could ask for anything as a parting gift. The minister, who was impressed by the king's bravery and righteousness, advised him to ask for the most unique thing in Bahubal's possession—the magical throne supported by the mystical statues of thirty-two nymphs. Accordingly, Vikram asked for the throne and Bahubal presented it to him without flinching for even a moment. He was finally permitted to depart, carrying blessings of just rule.

The reports of these events pleased Vikram's allies and robbed his enemies of peace. Apparently, he proved to be a deserving owner to the throne. His justice and generosity touched all, oppressors were punished, and peace and prosperity reigned. After some years, he launched the Vikram Samvat and wore the Ajeet Maal (the necklace of invincibility) which personified his resolve to be a just and generous protector of his subjects.[8]

Bhartari and the Life Elixir

After some time, Vikram handed over the kingdom to his younger brother Bhartari and left for the Kailash Mountains to live as an ascetic. In place of expensive jewels, a necklace of beads adorned his neck and his body was smeared with ashes. Bhartari was a kind and compassionate man and he tried his best to rule like his elder brother.

Meanwhile, in some jungle in the kingdom, a Brahmin was granted a magical fruit of immortality by a deity whom he had worshipped with remarkable devotion. Happy at this good fortune, he rushed home to share the precious boon with his wife. The poor woman opined that since eating the fruit would make them immortal, their sufferings due to penury would also become endless. Thus it would be wiser to present this invaluable fruit to the king and get wealth in return so that their naturally remaining

---

[8]Ibid., pp. 15–21.

days would be spent comfortably. Besides, the king was a well-wisher of his subjects and if he had a long life, a lot of people would benefit. Convinced by this argument, the man went to the palace to see the king. The monarch was pleased at receiving this rare gift and he granted the Brahmin handsome rewards of money and land.

Bhartari was quite clear that someone else deserved the fruit more than himself, and that was his beloved queen. He loved her so much that the thought of outliving her seemed torturous. He surmised that if the queen remained healthy and youthful, he would be happy for her—and that is what he desired the most. So he went to her chamber and gave her the blessed fruit. When the queen was informed that it was the elixir of life, she excitedly accepted the gift and promised to eat it.

The Kotwal (officer in charge of law and order) was the queen's paramour. Therefore, as soon as the king left, she immediately called for him. She felt the same things for the Kotwal that Bhartari felt for her, and so decided to pass on her husband's gift to her lover. She said to him, 'The Rajah has given me this fruit, and said that whoever shall eat it will become immortal. You are my beloved—eat it and become immortal. Then I shall be extremely delighted.'[9] When the Kotwal heard of the unique qualities of the fruit he could hardly believe his luck. Showing gratefulness for the queen's affection, he quickly accepted it.

The Kotwal actually loved a beautiful courtesan who was also his mistress. He took the fruit to her and said, 'I

---

[9] Ibid., p. 207.

have brought this fruit of immortality for you, eat it.'[10] Like the others, the courtesan too couldn't refuse the priceless gift of life. She thanked the Kotwal and was convinced of his love and loyalty—however, she was not sure about her own worth as the recipient of an unending life. Her fears were that as a courtesan she committed many sins and led a promiscuous life—she lived forever, she would be buried under an immeasurable pile of sins. In the end, hell would be her abode. Therefore, she should use the boon in such a meritorious way that her sins would be remitted and she would be remembered as a noble soul. After much deliberation, she decided to give it to the king for almost the same reasons for which the Brahmin had initially given it to him.

Bhartari granted an audience to the courtesan on her request and she respectfully presented the fruit to him. The king could hardly believe what he saw. His mind was befuddled with questions. However, he calmly enquired about the origin of the fruit. The courtesan said that the Kotwal had presented it to her and he may be able to explain the details. The king didn't want to face what this implied, but an enquiry was in order. So he accepted the gift and rewarded the courtesan for her confidence in his goodness. Thereafter he rushed to the queen's palace and asked her whether she had eaten the fruit—and his fears came true when she replied in the affirmative. He now showed the fruit to her. There was nothing more to say.

Bhartari suddenly felt powerless. He had realized that

---

[10] Ibid.

no matter how hard one tries, some things will remain beyond human control. He reflected, 'I bestowed my affections upon the queen, but she has given her heart to the Kotwal. I have not found an affectionate consort. Accursed be my existence and my reasoning power, if I recover! Accursed be the queen, the Kotwal, the harlot, and Cupid, who by his seductions infatuates the world... This world is transitory; the body, the intellect, wealth, nay life itself, are but illusions, and all these will cease to exist. As soon as man is born the angel of death begins to devour him. He wastes his life in vanity, imagining that everything belongs to him. Prosperity brings you friends, but adversity, no one shares with you. This world is an ocean, wealth is its water, and covetousness its fish—and no huntsman has ever been found who can kill and consume this fish.'[11]

Thus disillusioned by the unpredictability and falseness of the transitory world, Bhartari decided to walk away from its temptations. He ate the fruit lest it fall in the hands of some evil soul, and then left the palace forever to lead a life of rigorous asceticism. Eventually, Vikram returned to the kingdom and resumed his royal duties.

◆

Although this narrative conveys only two of the stories, an overview of all the thirty-two stories in *Singhasan Battisi* conveys that Vikram followed a middle path between

---
[11]Ibid., pp. 207–8.

renunciation and greed. His elder brother Sankh was ruthlessly ambitious, unnecessarily suspicious and greedy, and thus lost not just the throne but also his life. On the other hand, Bhartari, the younger one, was ruled by gullible emotionalism. Ignoring the fact that life is meant to be multidirectional and multidimensional, he held on to a single thought—that the world and everything within it is illusory and therefore one should distance oneself from it. Thus he renounced his responsibilities as a king. It was Vikram who struck a balance between ambition and asceticism. He worked to become powerful by fair means and then used that power to dispense justice and do good deeds. He made a positive difference in the lives of others and left behind a legacy of wisdom and breathtaking bravery. He was fearless but took calculated risks, lived by his words and was clearly just and generous by the standard and limitations of his times. It is professed that anyone who sat on his throne became supernaturally inclined to dispense absolute justice, the complexities of cases notwithstanding. In fact it was due to this quality that the elusive throne was rediscovered by Raja Bhoj. The report stating that when a cucumber farmer sat on a certain mound, he became capable of exemplary rightness and could administer justice with the expertise of an astute scholar, had led Bhoj to the lost throne. It is important to note that although the whole narrative is played out against the backdrop of the caste system, justice is still placed above all considerations. Vikram is celebrated for his equity, not his creed. Raja Bhoj was also a Kshatriya like him and a ruler as well, but that was not qualification enough. So he was not allowed by the supercelestial nymphs to sit on Vikram's mystical throne. His Kshatriya caste notwithstanding, the nymphs felt that he was not as pure-hearted and selfless as Vikram was. On the other hand, an innocent cucumber-growing farmer sat on the magical throne with equally magical ease. Anyone who selflessly intended public good, Kshatriya or non-Kshatriya, could sit on the throne. This symbolized that Vikram's sense of justice cut across caste and class lines. Perhaps that was what made Vikramjeet/Vikramaditya an undying legend.

Chapter II

A Persian Epic and a Betrayal of Epic Proportions

At length Rustem made a powerful effort and got Sohrab under him. Apprehensive however that he had not strength enough to keep him there, he plunged his dagger into the side of the unhappy youth, and fatality prevented all further resistance. Groaning heavily, the dying Sohrab said 'Alas! Came here in anxious search of my father, and it has cost me my life. But if thou wert a fish and sought refuge at the bottom of the ocean, or a star in the heavens, my father will be revenged on thee for this deed'—'What is thy father's name?' said the champion. 'His name is Rustem and my mother is the daughter of the king of Samengan.' On hearing these words, the world faded before Rustem's eyes and he fell senseless on the ground. After sometime he rose up in deep agitation and asked Sohrab what tokens he possessed to prove the truth of his assertion. 'For I am Rustem!' he said in agony. 'Alas!' rejoined Sohrab, 'The instinctive feeling was ever at my heart, but, wonderful to say it received no mutual assurance from thine! If a token is required, ungird my mail and there behold the amulet which my mother bound on my arm and which Rustem gave to her, saying that it would be of extraordinary use on a future day.' The sight of the amulet was an overwhelming blow to the father—he exclaimed in bitterness of soul, 'O cruelly art thou slain my son! My son! What father ever thus destroys his own offspring? I shall never be released from the horror of this dreadful crime and therefore better will it be that I put an end to my own existence.' But Sohrab dissuaded him from this resolution. 'It has been my destiny thus to perish, it can be of no avail to kill thyself. Let me depart alone and thou remain forever.' Rustem in utter despair flung himself on the ground and covered his head with dust and ashes whilst Sohrab continued writhing and fluttering like a bird from the agony of his wound... Rustem returned with the utmost speed and continued mourning intensely. 'Son of the valiant thou art gone, the descendent of heroes has departed. Right won't it be were I to cut off both my hands and sit forevermore in dust and darkness.' The body of Sohrab was then placed on a bier and there was nothing but lamentation... Alas! For that valour, that wisdom of thine alas! That sweet life thou wert doomed to resign. Alas! For the anguish thy mother must feel and thy father's affliction which time will not heal.

—FIRDAUSI, SHAHNAMA. A tragic sequence where Rustem unknowingly kills his own son Sohrab.[12]

---

[12]Firdausi, *Shahnama*, cf. *The Shah Nameh of the Persian Poet Firdausi*, (translated and abridged) James Atkinson, (edited) Rev. J.A. Atkinson, Frederick Warne and Co., London, 1886, pp. 139–41.

Timeline: Eleventh century

Backdrop: The *Shahnama* is one of the longest poems written by a single author. However, the length, as an achievement, is dwarfed before the narrative's unimpeachable style. Each word has been carefully selected from an oceanic vocabulary and used with laser-like precision. Written in the eleventh century, it is a compilation of the history of Persia from the earliest times. It accommodates myths, legends, mysteries and histories with seamless smoothness. The author tries to retain the conventions of basic chronology and divides the narrative into the mythical, heroic and historical ages, but poetic imagination often disregards chronology and frozen history. The life and times of heroes like Jamshed, Rustam, Sohrab, Afrasiyab and Isfendiyar, and kings like Alexander and Ardeshir, the Sassanian, etc are narrated with a paradoxical mix of moving realism and painstakingly ornamented poetic symbolism. The *Shahnama* impacted the writing style of the chronicles of the Sultanates which rose in the following centuries. Its capability of effective myth-making and ability to mesh myths and histories into the sociocultural fabric was such that some of the Turkish rulers of medieval India thought it prudent to trace their descent from the legendary heroes of Persia. In fact, the proliferation and impact of Persian myths in the Turkish and Afghan aristocracies was too deep to go unnoticed. The *Shahnama* played a critical role in persianizing many non-Persian powerhouses.

It was the yield of a steely resolve and thirty years

of laborious writing by Abdul Qasim Firdausi. He wrote it on the behest of Amin ul Millat Yamin ud Daulat Sultan Muhmud ibn Nasiruddin Ghaznavi. Mahmud is remembered for his grand capital Ghazni, immense wealth and equal miserliness. He raided Hindustan approximately seventeen times (1008, 1010, 1011, 1012, 1013, 1016, 1019, 1021, 1022, 1024, 1025, 1027 etc.) and is notorious for the destruction of the famed Somnath temple.

Satish Chandra estimates Mahmud as a bold warrior who single-handedly carved out one of the biggest empires in West and Central Asia. In the tenth century, Ghazni was merely a junction of trade between Khurasan, Transoxiana and India. The credit for its phenomenal rise as a rich centre of power and culture goes to Mahmud, who nurtured it with the wealth that he accumulated from his military exploits. His efforts at creating an aura around himself and his capital went far beyond military activities.[13] He was enthusiastic about contributing to the growth of the Persian renaissance which had originated in the time of the Samanids. The libraries at Ghazni and Samarqand were enriched by looting other libraries, and scholars were patronized to spin grand narratives of the court and the king. Al-Biruni was initially attached with the court at Ghazni but due to differences with the monarch, he left—and thankfully reached India to write the *Tahqiq ma li'l Hind*.[14] He, in fact, informs his readers that regions raided

---

[13]Satish Chandra, *Medieval India from Sultanate to the Mughals*, Part-I, Har-Anand Publications, Pvt. Ltd. New Delhi, 2001, pp. 19–21.
[14]Romila Thapar, *Somanatha: The Many Voices of a History*, Penguin Viking, New Delhi, 2004, p. 43.

by Mahmud suffered devastation and economic setbacks. The Turk raiders were as dreaded as they were hated. An exaggerated report states that Mahmud had captured about 53,000 prisoners after the campaign in Kannauj and they were sold at a price of two to ten dirhams per slave.[15] The Ghaznavid historian Utbi in his *Tarikh-i-Yamini* (1031) describes Mahmud's administration in Khurasan: 'Affairs were characterized there by nothing but tax levies, sucking which sucked dry, and attempt to extract fresh sources of revenue, without any constructive measure.' Hence, after a few years, there was nothing more to be got in Khurasan. 'Since water had been thrown on her udder, not a trickle of milk could be got nor any trace of fat.'[16]

The following section narrates the betrayal of the poet Firdausi by his royal patron Mahmud. He wrote the *Shahnama* with the hope of being rewarded by the rich Sultan, who had promised to pay him handsomely. But he didn't keep his word. In this regard, Abdul Qadir Badaoni cites Nuruddin Abdur Rahman Jami, a renowned mystic of medieval times:

> It is well to recognize merits
> For when the arched sky at last discharged the arrows of misfortune
> the glory of Mahmud passed away.
> Nothing remained in the world save only this saying:
> He recognized not the worth of Firdausi.[17]

---

[15]Ibid., p. 44.
[16]*Medieval India from Sultanate to the Mughals*, p. 21.
[17]Abdul Qadir Badaoni, *Muntakhab-ut Tawarikh*, Vol-I, tr. p. 32.

Thus Firdausi died a poor man only to be remembered as a great writer, and the Sultan died a rich man only to be remembered as a petty miser.

◆

It is believed that the Sassanian ruler Yezdjird had commissioned the creation of the great literary works of the Persian antiquity, with an eye to weave a rich tapestry of folk tales, legends, traditions and histories. This book was titled *Syur-al Muluk/Bastan Nama*. The first copy of the text was supposedly found in the plundered library of Yezdjird. However, interpolative postscripts to the text made additions to its volume and value. In the tenth century a king of the Samanian dynasty employed a poet named Dukki to render the voluminous *Bastan Nama* in verse, but unfortunately, only one thousand distiches had been completed when the man was murdered by his slave, and the work remained incomplete. Then, in the eleventh century, Mahmud ordered the poets in his employ to gain access to all the possible sources of the history of Persia and make a compilation of them with exemplary finesse. However, when a copy of the *Bastan Nama* came to his notice he realized that a lot of ground work for his pipe dream had already been done. After an intra-court competition between the poets in his employ, Abdul Qasim Hasan Unsari Balkhi, who had recomposed the amplified tragedy of Rustam and Sohrab, bagged the assignment of rewriting the whole history in verse.[18] He was entitled

---

[18]*The Shah Nameh of the Persian Poet Firdausi*, pp. xiii–xiv.

Malik us Shu'ara (King of poets) by Mahmud. However, destiny had her way and this enterprise was transferred to another poet: Firdausi.

Sources present different explanatory theories for this passover. One narrative claims that Firdausi had started versifying the *Bastan Nama* at Tus (his home town in northeast Iran) and had won quick acclaim for his well well-rounded compositions. When the good reviews of his work reached Mahmud's court, the Sultan invited him to Ghazni and granted him the prestigious assignment with an official and public promise that the writer would be paid at the rate of one thousand misqals (one misqal = $1^{3/7}$ dirhams = 6 dangs = 96 barley grains in weight. It is a weight used in weighing gold and also the name of a gold coin)[19] for one thousand distiches. Another account says that Firdausi's father Ishak Sharif Shah was a gardener at Tus, and he and his brother Mahsud were husbandmen. Vexed by an enmity with some local Mafioso, Firdausi left his home town. Although he tried to convince his brother to accompany him, the latter chose to stay.

To enhance the impressiveness of his talent, the account of his entry in Ghazni is often dramatized. It says that master poets Unsari, Usjudi and Farrukhi were in the midst of an intellectual get-together when they saw a stranger approaching them. To discourage some undistinguished fellow from joining their conclave, they said that they were using personification and rhyme to compose extemporary verses in praise of a woman, and only someone who could

---

[19]Cf. *Muntakhab-ut Tawarikh*, p. 25

keep pace with their instantaneous brilliance would be admitted to their club. Confident of his knowledge, Firdausi agreed to take the challenge. This exchange followed:

> Unsari: 'The light of the moon to thy splendor is weak.'
>
> Usjudi: 'The rose is eclipsed by bloom of thy cheek'.
>
> Farrukhi: 'The eyelashes dart through the folds of the joshun.'
>
> And Firdausi added: 'Like the javelin of Giw in the battle with Pashun.'[20]

The smug experts, who had planned to shake off their pursuer with ease, were in for a surprising reality check. They didn't know who Giw and Pashun were! So it became a case of ignotum per ignotius. However, they were learned enough to acknowledge their ignorance and ask. Firdausi's reply revealed his commanding knowledge of the *Bastan Nama*—and of course, his great literary skills were obvious. Living up to the true scholarly fashion they recognized his excellence and introduced him to the Sultan. Following is the first couplet that the poet composed in the Sultan's praise:

> The cradled infant whose sweet lips are yet balmy with milk
> from its own mother's breast lisps first the name of Mahmud.[21]

---

[20] *The Shah Nameh of the Persian Poet Firdausi*, p. xvi.
[21] Ibid., p. xvii.

So the flattered and exultant Sultan took an instant liking to the man whose words were the rarest kind of image intensifiers. And so, eventually, the project of versifying the *Bastan Nama* went to Firdausi. Aware of the latter's superiority, Unsari showed ungrudging grace and stepped back.

This version of the story seems to have been popularly accepted, since a painting of Firdausi's first meeting with the court poets of Mahmud finds place in the copy of the *Shahnama* commissioned by Shah Tahmasp I. The painting is dated 1532, and the painters are identified as Mir Musavvir and Dost Muhammad. The painters have highlighted the initial exclusion of Firdausi by painting him at a distance from the other three poets.

Bestowed with the title of 'Firdausi' (Heavenly) for bringing paradisal sophistication to the Sultan's court and enthused over the promise of 1000 miskals for 1000 distiches, Abdul Qasim set about writing his magnum opus, the *Shahnama*. Ahmad Mymundi, one of the ministers of Mahmud, was empowered to release the promised payout. Although he offered to give simultaneous installments with completion of portions, Firdausi requested a one-time payment. He planned to take all the money to Tus and earn blessings and merits by its virtuous expenditure.

As the work progressed, he became famous as a writer of enviable stature. Appreciation and gifts poured in, but the official payment was still on hold. In the meantime, Aiyar, one of the favourites of Mahmud, nursed a secret loathing for Firdausi. The egocentric minister was very touchy about his honour, and it deflated his vanity to see that the poet had not composed any verses in his praise. He appealed to Mahmud that Firdausi was a hypocrite who would promote schism and heresy by his philosophy. The Sultan's annoyance over this seems plausible, because Mahmud was at the centre of creating an intensified image of himself as an unbeatable enthusiast of Sunni Islam, while the *Shahnama*, being what it is was, was likely to have glorious images of Zoroastrian heroes as well. It is worth noting that during Mahmud's raids, his armies did not just harass the non-Muslims—they devastated the non-Sunni Muslims as well. The destruction of Mansura, a junction of Isma'ili Muslim traders, proves the point. On his way back from Somnath this centre was looted and many non-Sunni Muslims were killed. The local Isma'ili mosque was abandoned—in fact, at one stage, its destruction was also being contemplated.[22] The 'Sunni' mosque was put to use.

These attacks on non-Sunni Muslims were a manifestation of the fears of Sunni orthodoxy. The paranoia was probably born out of the fact that the ninth and the tenth centuries had witnessed the rise of many movements which challenged the formalism of the orthodox Sunnis. A few of these were politically hostile to the Khalifa of Baghdad, and that was an important point. The Shi'a, the Isma'ili, the Qarmatian, the Assassins, the Zanj people and the Druzes were some of them.[23] In Arabia itself it had taken Muhammad and the early Khalifas quite a while to convince the tribes to abandon all their earlier

---

[22]*Somanatha The Many Voices of a History*, p. 53.
[23]Ibid., p. 51.

conventions, which negated Islamic monotheism. It was not at all surprising the sects outside Arabia were still influenced by indigenous pre-Islamic belief systems like Zoroastrianism, Manichaeism and Buddhism etc. Then, of course, there was Sufism, which stood at the liberal end of Islamic mysticism and posed a serious challenge to the school of exclusivist Islamic jurists. The rivalry between Cairo and Baghdad over the legitimacy of Khilafat was bound to immediately impact the politics of Islam. This divisiveness cast a shadow on the lived religion and left its imprint in ways beyond the power of recording.

So, the Khilafat of Baghdad could use someone like Mahmud to fortify its position. He was, after all, an enterprising commander and a reasonably good consolidator. If Ghazni could be nurtured as a major centre of the eastern Islamic world, the Khilafat of Baghdad would improve its political sway. On the other hand, Mahmud, who had usurped his brother's throne, would have more than welcomed legitimization of his kingship by the Khalifa. By situating himself as the defender of Islam he would have fortified his position at home as well as in the larger context of the politics of the times. The titles that signified that he was a defender of Islam would have made recruitment in his armies easier, since religious enthusiasts were often blindfolded with ignorant zeal. Romila Thapar says:

> There may have been the echo of what has been postulated as a kind of cyclic movement in the epic of Firdausi, the *Shahnama*, anticipating the coming

of an Iranian and Islamic sovereignty through a king of the east. Possibly, the panegyrics on Mahmud may have led to the thought that he was such a king. This underlined his claims to legitimacy in ruling the empire of eastern Islam, more especially among the Turks who were impressed by the titles. The relatively obscure origins of his family would have made such legitimacy politically useful to his ambitions. His letters to the Caliph suggest a person who combines sycophancy with an aggressive self-righteousness, claiming that he has set forth exactly what God gave him the power to do in bringing victory to the Caliphate. The attempt to consolidate his holdings in the north-west India was also conditioned by the threat of the rising Seljuq Turks and of Byzantine power to the west. Later in the eleventh century, there was to be trouble from the further west in the assaults associated with the European Crusades.[24]

Celebratory references to Mahmud's attempts at thwarting anti-Sunni Muslim strongholds come from Farrukhi Sistani and Gardizi's *Zain al-Akhbar*. That was probably why his raids in India, and the whole of the Somnath episode, were escalated much beyond reality to create a larger than life image of this supposed champion of Islam. However, it is interesting to note that the man who was being projected as the epitome of a Sunni Muslim, had in fact made critical compromises for the sake of the undisturbed economic prosperity of the regions that he held. Bicultural coinage

---

[24]Ibid., pp. 52–3.

was important for the uninterrupted acceptance of the coins of the new regime. For someone who was acting as an agent of Sunni orthodoxy to have compromised on some of the core concepts of Islam for the sake of economic stability, is quite an eye-opener. In this regard a passage from Romila Thapar's *Somanatha: The Many Voices of a History* is worth citing:

> Ghaznavid control largely continued in the existing administrative system. Thus, Ghaznavid coins issued in the north-western India have bilingual legends written in Arabic and Sharda scripts. Some carry Islamic titles together with the portrayal of the Shaiva bull, Nandi, and the legend *Shri samanta deva*. The reference in the latter remains ambiguous. A *dirhem* struck at Lahore carries a legend in the Sharda script and a rendering in colloquial Sanskrit of the Islamic kalima and read*s: avyaktam ekam muhammada avatara nripati mahamuda*, 'the unmanifest is one, Muhammad is his incarnation and Mahmud is the king.' This was a considerable compromise since orthodox Sunni Islam, for whom Muhammad was a *paighambar*/messenger of God, would not have conceded that he was an incarnation of God. [25]

Therefore, while he might have made a compromise or two for economic gains, he would not have risked patronizing any narrative which even remotely tilted towards schismatic tendencies, as defined by Sunni orthodoxy. The idea of

---

[25]Ibid., pp. 42–3.

embracing non-Sunni legends did not easily fit in with Mahmud's larger agenda. Perhaps he never realized that anyone who hated and killed in the name of Islam, or widened the gaps between humans, was certainly missing some of the very basic values that Muhammad stood for.

Ultimately, the writer was summoned to the court and reprimanded. He tried to explain himself, but his entreaties were not able to purge the Sultan's mind of malice. Disillusioned with his patron but possessed by the desire to complete the majestic *Shahnama*, Firdausi kept working and his frenzied enthusiasm remained untamable. The consistency of his arduous writing finally paid off and after thirty years, the masterpiece was ready. With his pen, he had brought the past to life in a way that greatly inspired its readers. The emotive tragedies could deftly move one to tears, and the daring of the warriors could be an inspiration for the least aggressive.

Although the composition was priceless, the least that its author was expecting was the promised amount—which worked out to be a total of 60,000 miskals in this case. Ideally, the polishing of such a mammoth gem of history should have invoked pride and gratitude in its patron, but Mahmud was indifferent. It is not clear whether the non-payment was motivated by political considerations or the Sultan's well-known miserliness. Some accounts shift the blame to Aiyar, and they state that due to his manipulations 60,000 silver dirhams were sent to Firdausi instead of the promised gold. The receipt hit him like a thunderbolt. Angry and insulted by the outrageous betrayal, he felt shattered. In a state of delirious rage he immediately distributed the money amongst the people around him: a keeper of a public bath, a seller of refreshments and the slave who had brought the money, and somehow managed to wobble away. The shock had benumbed him.

The helpless man's reaction was reported as rebellion to Mahmud, and the enraged monarch ordered that his head should be crushed under an elephant's foot. Held in contempt and charged with devilry, Firdausi was amazed at the inverse relationship between his hopes and what he had attained. Abdul Qadir Badaoni records his disillusionment in the following verse:

> The auspicious court of Mahmud Zabuli is an ocean,
> An ocean such that no shore can be found for it!
> I went to the ocean—I dived but found no pearl
> The fault is my fortune's—not that of the ocean. [26]

He rushed to the court and implored the Sultan to forgive him. His case had become a classic tragedy worthy of being recorded in the *Shahnama* itself. A man who deserved praise and prizes was begging for his life! Motivated by human considerations—or maybe political ones—the Sultan spared him, but did nothing beyond that. The pardon saved his body, but his soul and spirit were sawed to bits. In retaliation, he wrote a scathing satire on the Sultan and added it to the very copy of the *Shahnama* which he had presented to the monarch. Thereafter he fled from Ghazni, because writing a satirical verse on the Sultan was like writing one's own death sentence; after all,

---

[26] *Muntakhab-ut Tawarikh*, p. 17.

the only weapon he was adept at using was a pen—and he had used it.

Firdausi's dreams of returning home as a rich and successful man were squashed. But as an asylum seeker he had the advantage of being an author of considerable renown, and was welcomed at Hyrcania, Rustemdar, Herat, Mezinderan and even Baghdad. Eventually, he did go back to Tus, and spent his last days there.

At some point of time Mahmud became conscious of the moral blunder that he had committed and tried to undo it. The descriptions of this change of perspective are many and varied. A generous account absolves him of all guilt by asserting that the Sultan didn't know that silver dirhams were being sent to the poet, but this seems rather unlikely. Besides, it was his personal responsibility to ensure that his promise was kept—because Firdausi had kept his, to the last detail. Rulers generally spent a lot in building an aura of majesty and grandeur around themselves and their court. The successful completion of the *Shahnama* project was meant to be a feather in Mahmud's cap, but it bled Firdausi's tears and stained the Sultan's pristine kingly robes. His lofty image had fallen, both in self and public estimation, and he expected it to spiral down further if he didn't take remedial measures. Thus Aiyar was banished from the court and a mission was dispatched to find Firdausi and hand over to him his due: the 60,000 gold coins, regal robes and apologies. Daulat Shah's biography gives another version—that when Mahmud was on one of his expeditions to Hindustan, someone recited a few couplets which the Sultan found to be exquisitely crafted.

Impressed, he asked for the author's name and lo! It was Firdausi.[27] In that moment, the Sultan saw beyond the veil of vanity and decided to redeem his error of judgement. However, there is no contradiction in the narratives about the fact that Firdausi died before the Sultan's apologies could reach him. His dead body, headed for the graveyard, and Ghazni's messengers, heading for his house, crossed each other at the gates of the city. Most sources state that his family didn't accept the offerings. So the rich Sultan, to this day, remains indebted to the poor poet.

Mahmud reigned for thirty-one years. For political reasons his serious—and final—illness was hidden for as long as possible. Aware that he may not survive for long, he desired to see his treasures, and accordingly all his valuable riches were placed in his sleeping chamber. Helpless in bed, he stared at them in despair. Despite their uselessness to him, he didn't give even a trifling to anyone.[28] He was not reconciled to leaving behind the wealth that he had gathered with all his might. The Sultan was inked with the label of being miserly, and this in itself was an apt punishment for the injustice done to Firdausi.

The idea of the circle of justice rests on the assumption that whatever goes around comes around. When promises are broken, the karmic chain of goodness is broken. We are so obsessed with protecting ourselves from other people that we forget to protect ourselves from ourselves.

---

[27] *The Shah Nameh of the Persian Poet Firdausi*, p. xxi.
[28] *Muntakhab-ut Tawarikh*, p. 31–2.

Firdausi's Satire on Sultan Mahmud

Know, tyrant as thou art, this earthly state
Is not eternal, but of transient date;
Fear God, then, and afflict not human-kind;
To merit Heaven, be thou to Heaven resigned.
Afflict not even the ant; though weak and small,
It breathes and lives, and life is sweet to all.
Knowing my temper, firm, and stern, and bold,
Did'st thou not, tyrant, tremble to behold
My sword blood- dropping? Had'st thou not the sense
To shrink from giving man like me offence?
What could impel thee to an act so base?
What, but to earn and prove thy own disgrace?
Why was I sentenced to be trod upon,
And crushed to death by elephants? By one
Whose power I scorn! Could'st thou presume that I
Would be appalled by thee, whom I defy?
I am the lion, I, inured to blood,
And make the impious and the base my food;
And I could grind thy limbs, and spread them far
As Nile's dark waters their rich treasures bear.
Fear thee! I fear not man, but God alone,
I only bow to his Almighty throne.
Inspired by Him my ready numbers flow;
Guarded by Him I dread no earthly foe.
Thus in the pride of song I pass my days,
Offering to Heaven my gratitude and praise.

From every trace of sense and feeling free,
When thou art dead, what will become of thee?
If thou shouldst tear me limb from limb, and cast
My dust and ashes to the angry blast,
Firdausi still would live, since on thy name,
Mahmud, I did not rest my hopes of fame
In the bright page of my heroic song,
But on the God of Heaven, to whom belong
Boundless thanksgivings, and on Him whose love
Supports the Faithful in the realms above,
The mighty Prophet! None who e'er reposed
On Him, existence without hope has closed.

And thon would'st hurl me underneath the tread
Of the wild elephant, till I were dead!
Dead! By that insult roused, I should become
An elephant in power, and seal thy doom—
Mahmud! If fear of man hath never awed
Thy heart, at least fear thy Creator, God.
Full many of humble, of imperial birth:
Tur, Selim, Jemshid, Minnehihr the brave,
Have died; for nothing had the power to save
These mighty monarchs from the common doom;
They died, but blest in memory still they bloom.
Thus kings too perish— none on earth remain,
Since all things human seek the dust again.

O, had thy father graced a kingly throne,
Thy mother been for royal virtues known,
A different fate the poet then had shared,

Honours and wealth had been his just reward;
But how remote from thee a glorious line!
No high, ennobling ancestry is thine;
From a vile stock thy bold career began,
A Blacksmith was thy sire of Isfahan.
Alas! From vice can goodness ever spring?
Is mercy hoped for in a tyrant king?
Can water wash the Ethiopian white?
Can we remove the darkness from the night?
The tree to which a bitter fruit is given,
Would still be bitter in the bowers of Heaven;
And a bad heart keeps on its vicious course;
Or if it changes, changes for the worse;
Whilst streams of milk, where Eden's flowrets blow,
Acquire more honied sweetness as they flow,
The reckless king who grinds the poor like thee,
Must ever be consigned to infamy!

Now mark Firdausi's strain, his Book of Kings
Will ever soar upon triumphant wings.
All who have listened to its various lore
Rejoice, the wise grow wiser than before;
Heroes of other times, of ancient days,
For ever flourish in my sounding lays;
Have I not sung of Kaus, Tus, and Giw;
Of matchless Rustem, faithful, still, and true.
Of the great Demon-binder, who could throw
His kamund to the Heavens, and seize his foe!
Of Husheng, Feridun, and Sam Suwar,
Lohurasp, Kai-khosrau, and Isfendiyar;

Gushtasp, Arjasp, and him of mighty name,
Gudarz, with eighty sons of martial fame!

The toil of thirty years is now complete,
Record sublime of many a warlike feat,
Written midst toil and trouble, but the strain
Awakens every heart, and will remain
A lasting stimulus to glorious deeds;
For even the bashful maid, who kindling reads,
Becomes a warrior. Thirty years of care,
Urged on by royal promise, did I bear,
And now, deceived and scorned, the aged bard
Is basely cheated of his pledged reward![29]

---

[29] *The Shah Nameh of the Persian Poet Firdausi*, pp. 341–3.

Chapter III

From Qutbuddin to Qutbuddin and the Bloodlust in Between

Sikandar who held sway over a world,
At the time when he was departing, and was quitting the world,
It could not be as he wished.
Though he would have given a world, could they have given him in return the brief respite of a moment...
Alauddin who struck his stamp upon the golden coin,
Subdued a world beneath the palm of his gold-scattering hand
By the revolution of the sky that stamp became changed,
But that gold remained the same in appearance
And you may see it now passing from hand to hand.

—ABDUL QADIR BADAONI, *Mutakhab-ut Tawarikh*[30]

---

[30] Abdul Qadir Badaoni, *Muntakhab-ut Tawarikh*, Vol-I, George S.A. Ranking (translation), Atlantic Publishers and Distributors, New Delhi, 1990 (reprint), pp. 268–69.

Timeline: Twelfth to fourteenth century CE

Backdrop: Towards the end of the twelfth century the Indian sociopolitical setup underwent strategic rearrangements. These alterations, rooted in the political rivalries of the various Rajput clans of north India, sprouted with the defeat of the Rajput monarch Prithviraj Chauhan at the hands of the Ghurid ruler Muizzuddin Muhammad Sam in the second battle of Tarain (1192). Numismatic evidence supports that after this defeat he was allowed to rule over Ajmer as a vassal of Muizzuddin, but was soon replaced by his son due to rebellion. He is remembered as a brave commander and a great patron of scholars. The ruler of Delhi, Govindraj Tomar, was probably a vassal of Prithviraj, and he died fighting in the second battle of Tarain. In 1193, the Tomar chief, who had probably accepted Turkish vassalage, was removed from the throne and thereafter Delhi became the base of all Turkish operations in India. After the battle of Chandawar (1194), the collapse of Kannauj (1198) and occupation of most of the impregnable forts like Bayana and Gwaliyar etc., the foundations of Turkish rule in eastern Rajasthan and upper Ganga valley became deep. Expansionist missions were sent to Gujarat in the west and Bihar and Bengal in east.[31] Thus, fuelled by the expeditionary efforts of the Turks, emerged an empire which was later christened Dilli Sultanate after the name of its nerve centre; Delhi of modern times.

---

[31]Satish Chandra, *Medieval India from Sultanate to the Mughals*, Part-I, Har-Anand Publications, Pvt. Ltd. New Delhi, 2001, pp. 26–7.

Although the Sultanate remained enshrouded in a seemingly stable facade, internal change was recurrent and often painful and bloody. The solidity of its structure lay in centralization and mechanisms of appropriation. The Iqtadari system (transferable land revenue assignments given in lieu of military service) bound the ruling classes and its intermediaries, tax collection, military organization and urbanization together in a single lineup. Ensuring a smooth flow of surplus from rural to urban areas was a major preoccupation of the governing bodies. However, about one-fourth of it leaked on the way, due to the puncturing effect of corruption. The ruling class was an assortment of people who could be classified on parameters of race, ethnicity, region, religion etc. A political incision was made to accommodate wealthy indigenous Indians therein. Therefore, besides the various classes of foreign settlers, the local rajas, ranas, rauts, khuts and muqddams etc. formed a band of exploiters—with the sultan at the top of this structure. The bandagaan/ghulaam (slave) sub-structure supported the Sultanate. Some of the so-called 'bandagaan' were men who had been acquired at a young age and were mentally drilled to be loyal to the sultan. They were coached in accordance with their aptitude. However, defeated rulers or chieftains were also branded with the designation of slaves. Some of them were experts of their craft, be it military strategy or economic management, and thus they rose to high positions despite being called slaves. Thus the title of banda/slave was not indicative of anyone's ethnic, social or economic background. Romila Thapar wonders whether some of the contempt for the Turk in Sanskrit sources emanates from the hurried presumption that the Turk banda was an equivalent of the Indian dasa.[32]

Perhaps the words 'sultanate' and 'sultan' emanate from 'tasallut', which means dominion/control/power. Two prominent features of this phase were abrupt and violent dynastic changes, and the intense thrust of the personal choices of the sultans on the governance of their times. Heredity as a determinant for political inheritance was discouraged in the early days of Muhammadan Islam. However, the ideal of democratic Khilafat was challenged by the notion of autocratic Mulukiyat. The strife between Hazrat Ali and Muawiya brought the debate on the administrative effectuality of the Khilafat to the battlefield. Later, the declaration of Yazid, Muawiya's son, as his successor reopened the doors for hereditary succession in Muslim polities—and this paved the way for ruthless autocracy, which generally goes hand in hand with undemocratic regimes. Prophet Muhammad's ideal of balancing power with piety was uprooted and finally washed away in the battle of Karbala with the blood of his own family. Once the watertight nature of his principles was unsealed, all kinds of ideas flowed in. Islamic ideals and Muslim practices started parting way and only a few could hold them together. Islam's demand for tolerance, equity, justice and piety was often denied by the very men who ruled in its name. In flagrant violation of Prophetic

---

[32]Romila Thapar, *Somanatha: The Many Voices of a History*, Penguin Viking, New Delhi, 2004, p. 41–2.

injunctions, Muslim rulers invoked Islam and defied Allah with the same panache.

The theory of Karma—that actions have sequential outcomes—is often invoked to explain events and reinforce goodness. All mainstream institutionalized religions and spiritual think tanks profess it with varying degrees of emphasis. They claim that every thought, word and action has a price, which has to be paid sooner or later. The narratives in this section support the philosophy of karma with terrifyingly smug ease.

Bloodline I: Sultan Qutbuddin Aibak (1206–1210), Sultan Aram Shah (1210)

At the time of Muizzuddin Muhammad Sam's death (1206), his favourite slave Qutbuddin Aibak was posted in Dilli as his viceroy. He was invited by the nobles at Lahore to declare his independence and ascend the throne. Eventually he was given a letter of manumission and a 'chatr' (umbrella; an insignia of royalty) by Muizzuddin's son Sultan Mahmud, and this facilitated an early breakup of Indian polity with Ghazni and Central Asian affairs. Thus with Lahore as his capital, he became the founder of what came to be known as the Dilli Sultanate. Entitled 'Lakh-Bakhsh' (endower of lakhs) he was famous for his generosity. Two other slaves of Muizzuddin became independent: Yalduz at Ghazni and Qubacha at Multan and Uchch respectively. Another development was the rising conflict between Khwarizm Shah, the ruler of Merv, and the famous Mongol ruler Chengiz Khan, who was making inroads in Transoxiana and Khurasan (1218). However, Qutbuddin didn't get much time to consolidate his empire, since his life was shortened by an accidental fall while playing chaugan (medieval polo). He was succeeded by his minor son Aram Shah, who was assassinated on the orders of Iltutmish, one of his bandagaan, who usurped the throne.

Bloodline II: Sultan Shamsuddin Abul Muzaffar Iltutmish (1210–1236), Sultan Ruknuddin Firoz (1210), Sultan Raziyatuduniya wal Din bint-us-Sultan Iltutmish-Sultan Jalaltudunya wad Din (1236–1240), Sultan Muizzuddin Bahram Shah (1240–1242), Sultan Alauddin Masud Shah (1242–1246), Sultan Nasiruddin Mahmud (1246–1266)

Iqtidar Husain Siddiqui asserts that Hasan Nizami and Muhammad Awfi, the authors of *Taj-ul Mathir* and *Jawami-al Hikyat wa Lavami-al Rivayat* respectively, were contemporaries of Iltutmish and they deliberately omitted mention of the coronation and the subsequent assassination of Aram Shah for fear of displeasing the reigning Sultan. Minhaj us Siraj Juzjani, the author of *Tabaqat-i Nasiri*, does mention Aram Shah as the immediate successor of Qutbuddin, but the fact that his patron was Sultan Nasiruddin Mahmud—one of the sons of Iltutmish—deterred him from stating clearly that the child was murdered.[33] However, Tabaqat—the first word

---

[33]Iqtidar Husain Siddiqui, *Authority and Kingship under the Sultans of Delhi*, Manohar, New Delhi, 2006, p. 82.

in the title of his book—has two meanings; 'chapters' and 'layers'. Living up to the second connotation, he delivers some pieces of information in such a way that they manifest only when one reads between the lines. Thus he suggests that Aram Shah was executed after Iltutmish came to Dilli. Thereafter, many young heirs were assassinated by usurpers. Iltutmish also adopted the Central Asian practice of engaging assassins to get rid of rivals through treachery, one by one, without engaging them in face-to-face combat. Thus many Muizzi and Qutbi bandagaan (loyalists of Muizzuddin and Qutbuddin Aibak) were assassinated by their own colleague Iltutmish, and their wealth was added to the royal treasury.[34] The Sultan married the youngest daughter of Aibak to nominally legitimize his usurpation.

In 1221, the danger of Mongol invasion loomed over the newly established Sultanate of Dilli because the fugitive ruler of Khwarazm, Jalaluddin Mangbarni, had arrived in India and had sought Iltutmish's support in fighting against Chengiz Khan. Iqtidar Husain Siddiqui cites Jalaluddin's message to Iltutmish as follows:

'The vicissitudes of fortune have established my right to approach thy presence, and guests of my sort arrive but rarely. If, therefore, the drinking place of friendship be purified upon either side, and the cups of fraternity filled to the brim, and we bind ourselves to aid and assist one another in weal and woe, then shall our aims and objects be attained; and when our opponents realize the concord

---

[34]Ibid., p. 52.

that exists between us, the teeth of their resistance will be blunted.'[35]

However, Iltutmish was too clever to be drawn into a conflict which didn't concern him directly, so the proposal was ignored but increased caution was maintained at the frontiers. On the advice of his wise wazir (chief minister) Nizam-ul Mulk Junaidi, he sent a humble request to the Khalifa of Baghdad for investiture. His plea was honoured and the Khalifa sent him many gifts: standard, ring, vest, turban, saddled camels, Arabian horses and robes of honour. To strengthen the military and administrative backbone of the sultanate, Iltutmish created a syndicate of officers known as the Bandagaan Turkishaan-i-Chahalgaani (forty Turkish families/slaves). They were homogenized by a common political agenda and were rightly designated as the Sutun-i Sultanate (pillars of the empire). Iqtas were downsized and centralization was emphasized.

It is believed that Iltutmish had nominated his daughter Raziya to be his successor, but after his death gendered arguments were used to sideline the princess. Finally, Ruknuddin Firoz, his drunkard and debauch son, succeeded him. Ruknuddin squandered the treasures accumulated by his father on prostitutes and vagabonds. His mother, Shah Turkan, was a Turkish slave girl. Vengeful, insecure and blinded by the glare of power, she ordered the assassination of the other children of Iltutmish. The Chahalgaani feared that the Sultan would take the empire down with himself and thus rebellions were sparked. Negotiations between

---

[35]Ibid., p. 57.

Raziya and the nobility were launched. They saw in her a puppet sultan whom they would control, and she saw in herself the rightful and confident heir of her father. Both blocs misunderstood and underestimated each other. Finally, Raziya's appeal to the people of Dilli shattered whatever little sponsorship Ruknuddin might have had, and the tables turned. Shah Turkan was locked up and Ruknuddin couldn't survive a single night in jail.

In the history of Muslim polities, Raziya was the first woman to be enthroned as a Sultan. It is notable that she was not entitled Sultana, the feminine word for Sultan—because this word didn't exist in her times! She began to weed out the disloyal nobles from the court. The hierarchy of the Turkish Bandagaan was ruffled by out of way transfers, promotions and demotions. Many non-Turks were inducted in state services and this made the senior Turkish nobility insecure. Scandalmongers sold the story of her fondness for an Abyssinian officer, Jamaluddin Yaqut, who was the amir-i-akhur (in-charge of the royal stable). She used his arm or shoulder to support herself while mounting a horse or an elephant. He was, in all likelihood, her confidant and a reliable commander. Her abandonment of purdahnashini (being veiled), use of manly garments in public, riding on elephants and holding an open court added further fizz to the wine.[36] However, the underlying issue was not her supposed affair. Amir Khusrau (a famous disciple of Shaikh Nizamuddin Auliya and the author of many important works, like *Ijaz-i-Khusravi*, *Khazain-ul*

---

[36]Ibid., p. 120.

Futuh and *Masnavi Dewal Rani Wa-Khizr Khan*) mentions that she was a competent ruler and her assertion of power turned many nobles against her, ultimately leading to a series of rebellions.[37] Raziya faced the crisis bravely and fought opponents on many fronts. Yaqut died fighting for her cause. Perhaps in an effort to forge a political alliance, she married Malik Ikhtiyaruddin Altuniya, the governor of Tabarhinda. However, their combined forces were defeated by Malik Bahauddin Balban, an ambitious member of the Chahalgaani who later became a sultan. Some sources state that she was killed by dacoits for loot, while others claim that Bahram Shah, a son of Itutmish, had her murdered to pave way for his own accession.

Through Raziya's murder, the Turkish bigwigs proved the point that they would not allow any non-Turks to rise as the crème de la crème of aristocracy, and that they were the kingmakers. Now power was decentralized and nobles managed their iqtas in an arbitrary manner. Thereafter, Bahram Shah and Alauddin Masud Shah, Iltutmish's son and grandson respectively, were seated on the throne and then deposed by the designs of the powerful nobles. The Chahalgaani's quest for potency undid everything that Iltutmish and Raziya had done to consolidate the power of the central government, and the mania subsided only when Nasiruddin Mahmud, an unassertive descendant of Iltutmish, was crowned as the Sultan. He wore regal apparel only for public appearances, and in private dressed in old

---

[37]Iqtidar Husain Siddiqui, *Composite Culture Under the Sultanate of Delhi*, Primus Books, Delhi, 2012, pp. 153–54.

rags. Unconcerned with affairs of the state, he spent his time in preparing manuscripts of the Quran. It is said that his handwriting was withdrawn from the public eye in such a way that no one could recognize it. The argument was that if it was recognizable, the Qurans copied by him would be overpriced.[38] However, it seems more likely that this had something to do with the Chahalgaani issuing orders under his seal and signature.

The two men who were particularly powerful in the early phase of Nasiruddin's reign were Qutluqh Khan, his stepfather, and Malik Bahauddin Balban, his father-in-law—both senior members of the Chahalgaani. However their internal differences opened the doors of admittance for many non-Turks, including local chieftains, to a relatively higher bracket of the governing class. For example, Balban employed Afghans, Khaljis and Siestani Pehlavans (wrestlers) as his personal bodyguards. Imaduddin Rayhan, an Indian eunuch, advocated Qutluqh Khan's case with the local chieftains, and thus he received the Khan's patronage and quick promotions. On the other hand, Balban was supported by his cousin Sher Khan Sunqar and Prince Jalaluddin. Ultimately Qutluqh Khan and the queen mother were chased out of the domains of the Sultanate, and they fled to Central Asia to save themselves. Now Balban assumed the title of Ulugh Khan Azam and became the Naib-i-Mumalikat (deputy sultan). He used the chatr as well which was an insignia of royalty meant to be an exclusive prerogative of a reigning monarch. A formal

---

[38]*Muntakhab-ut Tawarikh*, pp. 127–28.

permission for its use was probably taken from the Sultan, who in any case was a puppet in his deputy's hands. After getting rid of all his apparent rivals, Balban eliminated his 'master' and son-in-law and usurped the throne. Isami, the author of *Futuh us-Salatin*, and Ibn Batuta, the author of *Rihla*, report that Nasiruddin was murdered by Balban.

Iltutmish's fierce ambitions and ceaseless efforts notwithstanding, the Sultanate slipped out of the hands of his descendants. It is remarkable that the Sutun-i Sultanate Bandagaan Turkishaan-i Chahalgaani, a club of his own making, was the very agency that destroyed his progeny. Thus, his A-Team failed him.

Bloodline III: Sultan Ghiyasuddin Balban-i Khurd (1266–1287), Sultan Muizzuddin Kaiqubad (1287–1290) and Sultan Shamsuddin Kai Kaus (1290)

An influential insider of the Bandagaan Turkishaan-i-Chahalgaani, Balban surely knew just how the notorious clique worked. As a group, they had mugged Iltutmish's children and brought ruin to their master's family. So he decided to bring them down. He copied Iltutmish in consolidatory endeavours but avoided the mistakes made by the former Sultan. However, as time unfolded he made his own.

Balban invoked the Divine Rights Theory of Kingship and instituted Sajda (prostration before the sultan) and Paibos (kissing of the sultan's feet) as court practices. His kokaba and dabdaba (royal pomp and grandeur) were boundless.³⁹ A manipulated genealogical construct traced his ancestry to the legendary Turkish hero Afraisiyab. These measures were meant to indicate to his colleagues of the Chahalgaani that they were unimpressive subordinates. Gestures like power dressing, lack of approachability and unabated punishments further widened the schism. Malik Baq Baq, who was a Sar-i-Jandar (commander of the bodyguards), once killed one of his 'farash' (in-charge of floor coverings) in an inebriated state. The local 'barid' (intelligencer officer) and 'munhiyan' (spies) didn't report the matter due to fear of Baq Baq's wrath, but it was brought to the Sultan's notice by the deceased's wife. As a punishment, the barid's body was hung at the city's gate and Baq Baq was flogged to death in front of the plaintiff. Likewise, Haibat Khan, the muqta of Awadh, flogged one of his servants to death. The Sultan had him whipped five hundred times before handing him over to the victim's spouse to be killed. All arrogance vaporized, the fellow begged forgiveness of his servant's wife and managed to obtain it after paying her a sum of twenty thousand tankas. However, he was too ashamed to step out of his house after this defamation, and died of depression. Thus the Sultan woke up the elite, who had fantasized that they were above the law. He was projected as a protector of the poor and the oppressed, but rivals and rebels were beaten, blinded, starved, thrown from heights, drowned in water, put to sword or poisoned with relentless resolve. Sedition was curbed with an iron hand. His own past deeds were

---

³⁹*Authority and Kingship*, p. 67.

a reminder of what the seditious could be capable of, and that made him bizarrely insecure.

Sher Khan Sunqar, one of Balban's cousins, was a member of the Chahalgaani. He was an efficient commander and had been posted at the north-west frontier since the times of Sultan Nasiruddin Mahmud, to check Mongol insurgencies. He had also supported Balban in his struggle against Qutluqh Khan. However, he did not come to Dilli to pay tribute to Balban when he ascended the throne, because many members of the Chahalgaani had been bumped off on the Sultan's orders and he feared for his life. Who would have known better than Balban that Sher Khan's fear of the assassin's dagger was not far-fetched? And yet he took offence. The man's previous record of loyalty and efficiency was overlooked, and on the Sultan's order, one of his cup-bearers poisoned him. This treacherous killing proved very expensive in the long run. When Tamar Khan, who was sent as a replacement, failed at handling the Mongols, the Sultan perforce posted his favourite child on that turbulent front. This was the heir apparent, Khan-i-Khanan Prince Muhammad.

Prince Muhammad was a man of exceptional qualities. Amir Khusrau and Amir Hasan Sijzi (disciple of Shaikh Nizamuddin Auliya and author of *Fawaid ul Fua'ad*) praised his sophistication. It is believed that Shaikh Sadi of Shiraz was invited by him to Multan. He had plans of building an imposing Khanqah (hospice) for the Sufi. However, the request was turned down due to the saint's advanced age.

Fatima Hussain reports an interesting anecdote about the prince. He was married to a granddaughter of Iltutmish, and one night he divorced her in an inebriated state. In the morning, when the intoxication wore off, he regretted the *talaq* and wanted to revoke it. The qazi of Multan decreed that his remarriage with her would be permissible only after the lady was first married to someone else and then divorced by the second husband, to be married to the prince again. For once the Islamic personal law was not compromised to please the royalty. Accordingly, it was planned that the divorced princess would be married to the local Sufi Shaikh Sadruddin and he would divorce her the next day. However, the Shaikh refused to divorce her the night after the nikaah (the Muslim marriage ceremony), because the princess expressed her desire to spend the rest of her life with him. Prince Muhammad was enraged and pledged to avenge this breach of trust, but he was himself killed before he could.[40] The veracity of this account is debated, since such apocryphal incidents were often inserted into old texts to highlight the spiritual authority of saints.

Nevertheless, a posting at the north-west frontier was a challenging assignment and the prince proved to be brave and efficient. He visited his father as often as he could and gifted him priceless curios.

In those days, the region of Lakhnauti (Bengal) was infamous as the abode of sedition. Its prosperity and the distance from Dilli often enticed its governors to revolt. Greed once again pushed farsightedness into a corner

---

[40]Fatima Hussain, *The War that Wasn't: The Sufi and the Sultan*, Munshiram Manoharlal, New Delhi, 2009, p. 163.

and Tughril, the governor of Lakhnauti, took over the region and declared his independence. In 1276, an army was dispatched against him and the governor of Awadh, Aitigin Muy-i-Daraaz Amin Khan, was given the command. Although Amin Khan remained loyal to Balban and tried his best, he was defeated. An enraged Sultan sentenced him to the gibbet and his body was hung at the Badaun Gate for public display. The wise of the day said that this act of injustice would mark the beginning of Balban's end—and it did.

Bahadur, one of the best commanders of the central army, was now dispatched against Tughril, but he too failed. The second defeat of the imperial army further emboldened the rebel, and many military adventurers joined him. This stubborn insubordination was scraping the glitter of his aura of invincibility, and Balban was livid. He left the capital in charge of Fakhruddin Malik ul Umra, the Kotwal of Dilli, and pledged that he would return only after uprooting the resistance. His younger son, Mahmud Bughra Khan, was directed to join the royal army, and so Prince Muhammad's responsibilities in the north-west increased. After a frantic chase of almost two years (1280–1282) the rebel's head was cut off and brought to the Sultan. The man who shot the first arrow at him was honoured with the title of Tughril Kush (the slayer of Tughril). Tughril's family and supporters were hanged on gallows erected in the main market of Lakhnauti. A Qalandar (mystic) patronized by him was also hanged. So much blood flowed on the streets of Lakhnauti that many people fainted at the sight. Rebels belonging to Dilli and its neighbouring areas were imprisoned and taken back to be tortured and killed there, so that their example would be a deterrent to defiance and insubordination.

Reluctant to leave this hard-won recovery with any of his officers, Balban appointed his son Bughra Khan as the viceroy of Bengal. The prince was warned that if ever the thought of sedition crossed his mind, he should simply recall memories of Lakhnauti and recall its cleansing with blood. Ziauddin Barani, in the *Tarikh-i Firoz Shahi*, says that Balban's victory was indeed a defeat in disguise. He claims that when a triumphant victory is achieved despite unmerited violence, it is 'Istidraj'—the magic or hypnotic manipulation of a divine plot against an erring individual. In this, in spite of the use of sinful means, the end result initially turns out favourable for the sinner. Thus he never indulges in self introspection—until finally the divine plan fully unfolds and he is drowned in regrets that will never leave.[41]

After his return to Dilli, Balban was a placid, contented man. However, the treacherous vicissitudes of fate changed that. In 1285, Prince Muhammad was killed in an unexpected encounter with an advance party of Mongols, who were waiting in ambush. Living up to his reputation as a brave warrior, he died fighting. The Mongols carried away his dead body. His father-in-law, a non-Muslim chieftain named Rai Kalu, purchased it from them after much supplication and the payment of a huge sum of money,

---

[41]Ziauddin Barani, *Tarikh-i Firoz Shahi*, Ishtiyaq Ahmad Zilli (translation), Primus Books, Delhi, 2015, p. 59.

so that the beloved son of Balban could at least be given a decent burial.[42] It is reported that Amir Khusrau was also taken by the Mongols as a prisoner of war, but somehow managed to escape.

Balban was devastated. He would have been happy to trade his empire for his son's life, but that is not how the world works. At eighty years of age, he finally came face-to-face with the gross limitations of human power and planning. His treasures tormented him and the royal robes were stifling. No matter how many people prostrated before him, he knew that he was powerless; just another helpless soul. At night, in private, he lamented like a lunatic, tore his clothes, beat his chest and put dust over his head. This was Karma for Balban and it was just the beginning.

The late Prince Muhammad was now remembered as Khan-i Shahid (martyred prince). His son Kaikhusrau, who was being brought up in Dilli under Balban's guardianship, was now posted at the north-west frontier in his late father's position. He was also granted all the royal insignia which his father had. However, Balban was unable to reconcile with the loss of his beloved son. His neat plan of seating Prince Muhammad on the throne of Dilli and making Bughra Khan a sub-sultan of Bengal, independent but subordinate to Dilli's monarch, had failed right before his eyes. He probably held himself responsible for the prince's death because he had got Sher Khan murdered and eventually sent Muhammad in his place. He knew that regret and depression had drafted his death sentence, and therefore

---

[42]*Composite Culture*, p. 35.

Bughra Khan was ordered to come post-haste to Dilli. Balban's health improved on seeing his son, but the latter's attachment to Lakhnauti prevented him from staying by his father's side for long. Sly and defiant, he left Dilli, Balban's entreaties notwithstanding. This was a great shock for the ailing Sultan, and his condition worsened. Fearful of a blitz on a vacant throne, Balban named Kaikhusrau as his successor. However, shady political designs began even before he was buried. Some of Khan-i Shahid's influential enemies snubbed his son's claims and raised Bughra Khan's son Kaiqubad to the throne. Kaikhusrau was dispatched to Multan. It is possible that Bughra Khan was also a party to this layout, because now the Sultanate was practically divided between him and his son. Balban's will was not implemented despite him being a man who claimed to be the shadow of God on earth—'Zill-i-Allah'.

Within a year of Sultan Muizzuddin Kaiqubad's accession, many of the Balbani bandagaan were sacrificed on the altar of suspicion. The seventeen-year-old Sultan was like an untrained gladiator thrown into an arena full of wild animals. Under the supervision of his grandfather he was being trained in everything from archery to literature, but the thunderous political developments changed the course of his life. Now he floated in a sea of pleasures, unmindful of what awaited him at the shore of such waters. A grand palace was constructed at Kilukheri and he shifted there with all paraphernalia in tow. Treasures, accumulated over the years, were consumed like air and Balban's principles of strong governance vaporized. Fakhruddin Malik-ul Umra, the aforementioned Kotwal of Dilli, was an old loyalist of

Balban. His nephew and son-in-law Nizamuddin rose to quick prominence due to this connection and his personal talent for manoeuvring. The Balbani bandagaan anticipated that Kaiqubad's fragile hands would not be able to hold the sands of power for long, and therefore some of them joined Nizamuddin, while the more ambitious ones nosed around the empire to bite off whatever they could.

The first victim of Nizamuddin's cunning was Kaikhusrau. He impressed on the Sultan the need to eliminate his cousin, who had a convincing claim to the throne by virtue of being the dauntless Khan-i Shahid's son and Balban's choice as his heir. The Sultan was not smart enough to see further than his nose. Consequently, the unsuspecting prince was summoned from Multan to be assassinated in Rohtak. In what the Sultan saw as a move ensuring the surety of his crown, others noticed a sure-fire way of losing his head. Khwaja Khatir, the wazir, tried to make him see some sense, but the poor fellow was falsely accused of some crime and paraded around on a donkey. Thereafter, the terrified Balbani nobles resolved to keep out of Nizamuddin's way.

His next quarries were the Mongol converts who had settled in Dilli and were active participants in palace politics. By fabricating intelligence reports that portrayed them as a comradely military group, he set them up as a threat to the sultanate and the Sultan's life. Hence, one day, all of them were invited to a feast where they were poisoned and slaughtered while intoxicated. Their mutilated and blood-soaked bodies were thrown into the Yamuna. Further, their houses were looted. The Balbani nobles who were related to them by marital ties were transferred to distant places to diffuse tension. Malik Shahak, the Amir of Multan, and Malik Yuzaki, who was the Arz-i-Mamalik (muster master), expressed their antipathy to such violence—and as punishment, they too were bumped off.

As the Haakima (governess) of the harem, Nizamuddin's wife became a dominant figure in the royal household and the Sultan addressed her as 'mother'. However, her father, the ninety-year-old Kotwal, was very uncomfortable with these developments. Barani writes that he reminded Nizamuddin that the latter wasn't brave enough to even hit a jackal with a stone or a vegetable vendor with the leaves of an onion—how could he then depend on men handicapped by vanity, greed and lust to be his soldiers? Or was he expecting men who combed their beards and wore gold bands and heavy perfumes to fight a war for him? If so, he was indeed chasing a mirage and imperilling the lives of his family and himself. He said:

> I have brought you up and you are like a son to me. My father and I have held the post of Kotwal of Delhi for eighty years and since we avoided meddling in the affairs of the state, we have remained and still continue to remain out of harm's way... Relinquish this mad idea of kingship as it has no relationship at all with us and we are not worthy of it. The robe of kingship fits those intrepid people who are capable of breaking ranks of the enemies and who could wreak havoc with the armies by their courage and bravery. It does not fit us who could not even make a horse gallop; neither do we

know how to send an arrow, use a lance or unsheathe a sword. Moreover we have never faced a battle, have never come out of the palace and led an expedition... If you do not remove this wicked idea that has settled in your mind because of your proximity with the king... our family will be annihilated and your design would come to nothing.

O young fox, why did you not remain sitting in your place, You entered in a brawl with the lion and met with your nemesis.[43]

Everyone who heard of this sagacious advice appreciated the Kotwal's farsightedness; everyone except Nizamuddin, for whom it was meant. In fact, he was so deep in the pit of high-pressure politics that any attempt to pull out would have ripped him apart. Thus he dived deeper into it. Reports of Kaiqubad's inability to recognize nightmares dressed as daydreams filtered into Lakhnauti and showed Bughra Khan that it was time for him to intervene. Accordingly, a meeting of the Sultans was fixed at Awadh; near the banks of Saryu.

Both parties arrived with majestic paraphernalia. Regal tents were pitched on either side of the river and a few days passed in finalizing the modalities of the conference. Although the father and son were disinclined to formalities, Nizamuddin was insistent on it. Protocol forbade the Sultan of Dilli to go to meet the ruler of Lakhnauti, because the later was supposed to be his subordinate. Therefore Bughra

---

[43] *Tarikh-i Firoz Shahi*, pp. 82–3.

Khan gracefully agreed to cross over to meet his son. An auspicious day chosen by the astrologers was fixed for the meeting. Bughra Khan humbly performed the 'zamin-bos' (kissing the ground in someone's honour) at four places and finally reached his son. On sighting his father, the Sultan forgot Nizamuddin's state etiquette tutorials. He rushed from the throne and fell at Bughra Khan's feet. The father and son embraced each other and cried. The day was marked by joyous celebrations and unprecedented charity.

Thereafter, they met many times, but Nizamuddin's serpentine spies kept slithering around them. Through indirect references, Bughra Khan tried to warn Kaiqubad of power vampires acting loyal to him. To diplomatically advise his son to be alert of usurpers, he mentioned that if a king fathers many sons, he himself becomes their assassin, because most of them do not survive fratricidal strife within the royal circle. Such is the power of power itself, that it shreds the fabric of trust thread by thread. Kaiqubad was reminded that he had inherited the sultanate and hadn't established it through his own merit—and perhaps that was why he didn't value it enough. With his perpetual and shameful orgies he was not only digging out the roots of the sultanate, but was also being a Judas to his own body and soul. Bughra Khan even pointed out that the assassination of Kaikhusrau was a personal and professional mistake and instead of eliminating efficient men, he should use them as pillars to support his government. On the day of the final parting, amidst tears and sighs, he managed to whisper in his son's ear that he should get rid of Nizamuddin at the first possible opportunity. Kaiqubad's promises to make amends notwithstanding, Bughra Khan prophesized his son's doom. Indeed, he had rightly assessed that the Sultan was unconscious of the deadly maze he was lost in, like a damned person in denial.

Kaiqubad had pledged to give up his substance abuse and sexcapades. However, the very sight of a sensuous youth unfroze his resolve. The nymphean appeal of prostitutes pushed him into an orgy of self-destruction. In fact, following his example, the whole entourage indulged in all kinds of impropriety. As a residue of Balban's sway, the Sultan received tributes from local rulers but not a single tanka of it made it to the royal treasury—because all of it was squandered over the course of the journey. In this regard, Ishtiyaq Ahmad Zillis's translation of the *Tarikh-i Firoz Shahi* reads as follows:

> Sultan Muizzuddin returned from Awadh towards Delhi. For only a few days he respected the advice of his father and did not go near the assemblies of indulgence and merrymaking, did not consume wine, did not listen to music and did not summon beauties to his presence. Since the fame of his rewards, excessive indulgence in pleasure-seeking and merrymaking, elegance of his nature, the goodness of his temperament had spread far and wide and his love for beauty and his gallantry for women had become known to people at large, the infamous men and women with a view to make a presentation to the king trained comely, beautiful and delicate girls, who were like mines of loveliness with amorous gestures and blandishments, mirthful

and experienced in the art of singing, playing of *rubab*, recitation of *ghazals,* making pleasantries and jokes and playing chess and dice. These moon-faced beauties, everyone of whom was enough to tempt an entire city and seduce the whole of the world, were brought up with great care and even before the bud of their breast had not yet blossomed in the garden of their youth, were trained in horsemanship, playing golf, using lances with much smartness and alertness. These seductresses were taught many other charming and alluring tactics that could compel a pious man to put off the *Zunnnar* (the Brahmanical thread) and lead the devout to the tavern. The slave merchants of Hindustan taught the cypress-like boy slaves and moon like girl maids Persian and music and adorned them with gold and jewelry and clothes made of brocade and embroidery and taught these lovely playful things etiquettes and manners and ways of service at the court. Beardless and handsome slave boys whose peers could not be found and girl maids of unparalleled beauty were decorated like newly-wed bride. Expert musicians and singers had composed all sorts of Persian and Hindavi songs and praises of the Sultan...jesters and *bhand*s who could send those weighed with grief into raptures and make the stomachs of the happy writhe with pain due to excessive laughter, all of these arrived... The distillers of Kol and Meerut having distilled fragrant intoxicating liquor and two three years old wine stored in flagons, brought them for presentation before the king... In spite of the fact that the Sultan felt deeply attracted towards these moon-faced beauties and his heart went out to them, yet due to the shame of the advices of his father which had become known throughout the army, he controlled himself. One day during the journey, a young boy like a piece of the moon, saucy and amorously playful, temptation and allurement personified, unrivalled in comeliness, wearing a cloak inlaid with gold putting a gilded quiver across the waist from which a tail of the tiger was suspended, putting on a kingly cap that came till the tip of the ear, riding a dark reddish brown horse raising its tail, with gilded accourtrement and a coat of mails with a breastplate, galloping like hunters with a black flag suspended with the neck of the horse –that rider of the arena of loveliness came out of the camp. He galloped the horse, twisted it and made it run towards the imperial cavalcade. Those who were near the Sultan and those who were marching with the cavalcade thought that perhaps some prince is pursuing a game whose loveliness, delicacy, smartness and gait dazzled the eyes of the spectators. That bewitcher of the souls and seducer of the hearts came from in between the ranks like an arrow, returned and arrived in front of the royal cavalcade. The guards, the sergeants and *naqib*s who were marching in front of the royal *chatr* with *chaqmaq* (flint) and maces in their hands were so overwhelmed with his grace and beauty that they could not prevent him from coming near the royal *chatr*. In a twinkle of the eye that embodiment of loveliness reached the presence of the Sultan, dismounted from the horse and rolled on the ground in front of him and recited this verse in the most melodious and sweet voice.

If you put your feet on our eyes,
We will put the pupils of our eyes in the way so that you may walk over them—Oh you with a form like cypress made of silver are heading for the desert,
You are indeed a great promise breaker that you are going there without us.

After reciting these verses he said to the Sultan with many blandishments and coquetry, 'So many of us lovely and amorous have come from such long distances to have a glimpse of the king and you are totally shunning us. Don't we deserve even a glance?' From the charm of this destroyer of houses and from the blandishments of that essence of repose of the souls, the king was totally infatuated and enamored. He was so completely bewitched with his loveliness and charm and his way of conversation that he wanted to come down from his horse and take him into embrace. The sight of that breaker of repentance and the modulations of his soul nourishing voice took him over and he lost patience. Due to total lack of self-control he immediately called for wine, took the royal goblet in the hand and drank it facing the moon-faced and cypress-statured one... The spectators were astonished by the sight of such exceptional beauty and delicacy of his voice and very much longed to hand themselves over to him. He galloped the horse and took the bow in the hand, joined the arrow with it and leapt under its wings. The sight of such charm sent the troops around the king in a tizzy, the reigns were abandoned and both eyes were fixed on him. As soon as the Sultan alighted for the stay, a pleasure party was organized. He summoned the embodiment of temptation and seduction and with hundreds of longings said to him: 'We wish to drink the wine from your hand and today you should be the cup-bearer of this assembly of ours.' That sweetheart responded with coquetry:

Though we are more beautiful than the moon, still we are the slaves of the slaves of the king.

Having said this he filled the goblet and gave it to the Sultan. The Sultan while taking the goblet from his hands and while holding it in his hands continued to remain immersed in beholding his world-illuminating face and recited this couplet:

When the cup comes to me give to those who are still sober, Leave me so that I may continue to remain keeping my eyes fixed on the eyes of the cup-bearer.

That cup-bearer who like the cypress in stature with silver color of the body, employing all the blandishments, put his head on the ground knitting his eyebrows with all the lovely gestures and said in a softer voice: 'O King of the world drink, O King of the world drink.' The Sultan said: If you are willing to act as cup-bearer for us who says that wine is prohibited... On the orders of the Sultan 2000 tankas of silver were brought and scattered on the head of that cypress of the garden of beauty. Laughing and jocularly he submitted that this *nisar* (offering) rightfully belonged to those who reared a moon like me for a king like you and who are still waiting on the door to be admitted in. Sultan asked is there anyone among them like you? He replied O King of the world, mothers give birth rarely to someone like me but all of them are like Parveen (Pleiades) in the attributes of beauty who outwit the Farzin (Queen of the chess) of the sky and since they sing very well, Zahra (Venus) is obliged to stamp its feet on the ground (out of jealousy). If they are brought in the auspicious presence of the king of the world, the melodious voice of their singing would bring the birds from the air to the ground and walls and doors will begin to dance. Orders were issued to bring these people in. When they looked on them they found that each one of them was more handsome and comely than the other and had a more melodious voice than the other. When they began to sing and stamp their feet the spectators were dazed by their good looks and blandishments. The Sultan was wonderstruck by the loveliness of these wonton-eyed ones and the subtleties of their talk, the stamping of their silvery feet and their playing of the *rubab* made him totally forget the advices of his father. He totally broke the thread of counsels and put aside the tablet of admonition and became engrossed in indulgence day and night with these breakers of the repentance.[44]

---

[44]Ibid., pp. 95–9.

Happy at the fruitlessness of Bughra Khan's visit, Nizamuddin waited for his chance to strike, but disease struck Kaiqubad before he could. Regret is a tormentor that makes people pray for dementia, and illness often prompts self-introspection. Therefore, as the infirm Sultan lay in bed, realization of his lapses haunted him. As a measure of damage control, he disaffiliated Nizamuddin and transferred him to Multan—without considering the administrative vacuum his departure would create. After all, Nizamuddin had already put down most of the competent officers who had the potential to replace him. Nevertheless, his supposedly unsinkable ship had now hit an iceberg. He knew that in his absence, his family would be vulnerable in Dilli. Nor was it safe for him to travel. Indeed, who could have estimated the perils better than him? He had designed numerous high-profile assassinations on highways. Thus, he delayed going to Multan on various pretexts. Yet, perhaps a city which had witnessed so many executions arranged by him was destined to testify to his as well. On the Sultan's order, he was invited to the palace and served poisoned wine. The toxicity of the poison was such that he died the same day.

Now the ailing Sultan summoned Jalaluddin Khalji, the royal deputy at Samana, to take over as the Arz-i Mamalik at the centre—but little did he know that he had invited his assassin and successor. Life often emulates the classic features of dramatic irony. Kaiqubad's intellectual awakening was preceded by physical paralysis. He suffered incessantly as political predators prayed for his end. Kilukheri, his paradise, had perished and been reincarnated as hell.

The Balbani and Muizzi nobles brought Kaiqubad's infant son out of the harem and placed him on the throne as Sultan Shamsuddin Kai Kaus.[45] It was obvious that the three-year-old Sultan was not going to actually rule. His accession was designed to curb the growing ambitions of Jalaluddin Khalji, who had been entitled 'Shayista Khan' and given the post of 'Wazir' by Kaiqubad before being totally incapacitated. Secondly, a baby Sultan was the best bet for the ambitious nobility, which ran an egocentric club. A new court called 'Chabutra-i-Sultani' came up and the stars of this galaxy of power revolved around it. However, none of this could check the continuous upsurge of Jalaluddin's military influence, which was becoming intolerable for the Turkish nobility.

According to early Chinese and Arabic sources, the Khalijis were Turks by origin, but after being driven out of their homeland they settled near Ghazana in areas around present-day Afghanistan. Medieval sources like the *Tarikh-i Fakhr-i Mudabbir* and *Dastur-ul-Afazil* also list them among Turkish tribes. The *Zafan-i Goya* states that Khalaj belonged to the Turks, and the region was famous for the good looks of its inhabitants and the fragrant musk found there. It seems that over a period of time, their complexion became darker than the central Asian Turks and they also developed a different dialect.[46] Perhaps they were not as persianized as the other Turks were, and thus were considered inferior. Nevertheless, they were

---

[45]*Muntakhab-ut Tawarikh*, p. 229.
[46]*Authority & Kingship*, pp. 91–3.

dauntless warriors. Tensions between the bands of Khaljis led by Shayista Khan and the Balbani nobles rose to such an extent that a combat between the two parties seemed imminent. In an effort to defuse the situation, the Balbani and Muizzi loyalists displayed a paralyzed and seriously ill Kaiqubad from a summit of the Kilukheri palace. They placed a royal umbrella over the dying man's head and paid obeisance to him. However, the truth was that both Kaiqubad and Kai Kaus were make-believe sultans, and Jalaluddin was not buying any fantasies.

Eventually Kai Kaus was kidnapped by the Khaljis and carried away to their military camp at Baharpur. Malik Aitmar Surkha, who was the face of Turkish opposition, pursued them, but was slain by Jalaluddin's son Ikhtiyaruddin Khalji. Malik Aitmar Kachchan, who was the other active opponent, had already been killed. Malik ul Umra Fakhruddin, the old Kotwal of Dilli, enjoyed a lot of trust and goodwill from the locals. His sons were kidnapped by the Khaljis to be used as pawns to steer favourable negotiations.

The tragic circumstances of Balban's descendents caused quite an uproar in Dilli. Furious crowds, armed with whatever weapons they could lay hands on, swarmed through the twelve gates of the city. They assembled at the Badaur Gate and resolved to die for the life of baby Kai Kaus. Now the Kotwal was forced by the Khaljis to use his wherewithal to disperse this wrathful mass. His failure would have caused the killing of his hostage sons. Years of his service and empathy with the locals paid off. By his speech, smoldering hearts were dampened and the multitude dispersed. Perhaps they never realized that the man who addressed them that day was not the Kotwal—he was just a helpless father.[47]

Kai Kaus was closely guarded by Jalaluddin's most trusted men. Surprisingly, among them was also Malik Chajju, a nephew of Balban. Now, an assassin was sent to Kilukheri to murder a comatose Kaiqubad. The villain wrapped him in a sheet, gave him a few kicks and blows and tossed him in the Yamuna. Another account says that he was imprisoned and died of hunger and thirst.[48] In the subsequent negotiations, the Kotwal was instrumental in the allotment of the rich province of Kara (Allahabad) to Malik Chajju and Jalaluddin Khalji was made the wazir' (prime minister) of the young Sultan Kai Kaus. It was a convenient arrangement, because Malik Chajju, who could have laid a claim to becoming the infant Sultan's guardian by virtue of being his relative, was bought off—at least for the time being. For a month or two, Jalaluddin himself carried the Sultan to the court and conducted all affairs of governance in his name. He probably wanted people to recover from their recent concussions before he dropped the next bombshell. Finally, one day, Jalaluddin seated Kai Kaus on his own horse and took him to Kilukheri. The child was killed there. The Wazir imprisoned his corpse in a grave and set his soul free.

---

[47]*Muntakhab-ut Tawarikh*, pp. 228–29.
[48]Ibid.

Bloodline IV: Sultan Jalaluddin Firoz Shah Khalji Ibn Yagrash Khalji (1290–1296), Sultan Ruknuddin Ibrahim (1296), Sultan Alauddin Muhammad Shah Khalji Sikandar-i Saani (1296–1316), Sultan Malik Shahabuddin (1290), Sultan Qutbuddin Mubarak Shah Khalji (1316–1320)

It is indeed true that life is full of surprises, but time often mitigates the element of surprise by turning every change into the new normal. The Khaljis, whom the Turks ridiculed and the locals looked down upon, not only became rulers, but one amongst them is remembered in History as an administrator of matchless repute. Thus Jalaluddin Khalji became the pioneer of the Khalji Revolution. The metamorphosis began with the rise of this new ethnic group and climaxed with the ruthless autocracy of Alauddin Khalji.

The grid of Jalaluddin's power had seven nuclei: himself, his three sons—Ikhtiyaruddin Khan-i-Khanan, Arkali Khan and Qadr Khan, his two nephews and sons-in-law—Alauddin Khalji and Ulugh Khan, and a loyal comrade, Ahmad Chap. The rising of Dilli's population in favour of Kai Kaus was still a recent affair, and therefore Jalaluddin didn't deem it safe to go to Balban's Kushak-i Lal (Red Palace) straight away. Instead, Kilukheri was refounded and new palaces and gardens were commissioned by the Sultan. The nobility believed that the place was ill-omened due to the fates of its founder Kaiqubad and his son. Besides, it was rumoured to be haunted by restless spirits. Nevertheless, they moved there to please the Sultan. Residences and markets came up and things began to normalize. When his accession had sunk into the heads of the citizenry, he finally held court at the Kushak-i Lal. The realization that he was sitting on the throne before which he had prostrated for years was pure euphoria to him. However, what he saw that day was nothing but a war zone disguised as paradise.

Malik Chajju, Balban's nephew, who had received the governorship of Kara as the settlement deal, revolted. Many Balbani and Muizzi bandagaan sided with him. It was important to curb the rebellion promptly, because it had unbounded misgivings about the Khalji takeover. The best men were deputed for the task and, under the leadership of Arkali Khan, the rebels were put to rout. Most of them, including Malik Chajju, were arrested. They were presented, dishevelled and dispirited, before the Sultan. It was expected that they would be humiliated, tortured and killed. However, anticlimactically, the Sultan sent them to the Tashtdaars (those who poured water) and Jaamaadars (keepers of robes) to be bathed, perfumed and dressed in fineries.[49] He had decided to pardon sedition, which was considered to be totally unforgivable. Perhaps this was an attempt to harness the acceptance and support of the senior Turkish ruling houses. Nevertheless, the anomaly distempered the gangbusters of the Khalji camp—they now perceived the Sultan as weak and not worthy of their loyalty. Ahmad Chap reminded his patron that a brutal judiciousness is essential for governance and like punishments, forgiveness should also have limits. The

---

[49] *Tarikh-i Firoz Shahi*, p. 114.

Khaljis became agitated at the belief that had the Turks been in their place, they would have slaughtered the rebels to the last man. The Sultan's atypical leniency created differences of opinion, and he was soon challenged and out-competed by the young Khaljis who had lost confidence in him.

The prosperous iqta of Kara was now assigned to Alauddin Khalji. Having brought him up himself, the Sultan loved and trusted him. However, Alauddin was a bitter man who was trapped in a bad marriage with the Sultan's daughter. Barani writes of his strained relationship with his wife and mother-in-law, but does not specify the reason for the hostility. Perhaps the ill temper and ruthlessness that Alauddin displayed right through his career, and his mother-in law's domineering nature, almost answer that question. Surely he might have found it difficult to ill treat the princess—and therefore becoming a powerhouse equal to or bigger than her father seemed like a feasible remedy for his heartache. The mildness of Jalaluddin's administration convinced him of the realism of his dreams. The Sultan forgave hardened criminals, thieves and fraudsters on promise of reformation. Rebellious officers were regularly pardoned and a lenient view was taken when dealing with intermediaries like zamindars, khuts etc. His policies were hardly conducive to incorruptibility.

The elite had heard on the grapevine that Alauddin was exploring means of breaking free of his royal spouse. His high-flown ambitions could barely be hidden under the cloak of tranquility. Thus he constantly attracted money and men to thicken the broth of sedition. Paradoxically, while Jalaluddin forgave shady and nefarious offenders, the one man whom he chose to punish on mere suspicion alone was a Sufi mendicant, Sidi Maula.

It is believed that Sidi Maula had visited Shaikh Fariduddin Ganj-e Shakar at Ajodhan on his way to Dilli, and that the Shaikh had given him a doom-laden word of warning—to be distant from persons of royal blood and powerful officials of the court. He asked Sidi to consider their visits to his house as calamities. This was not just important for elevation of spiritual rank, but was essential for the safety of the dervesh's life, given the political context of the times.[50] Accordingly, in the early days of his stay in the capital during Balban's reign, he kept a low profile, but became rather prominent in Kaiqubad's period. He was a celibate who led an austere life. His asceticism and abstinence were inhumanly extreme, but he never visited the mosque for the Friday congregational prayers. He didn't have any known sources of income like an Iqta or Futuh (unsolicited charity) but still had enough money to build and run a majestic khanqah. In his khanqah a thousand mans of fine flour, five hundred mans of freshly skinned meat and three hundred mans of sugar were used daily, to prepare meals for the crowds that thronged at its door. It was rumoured that he was an alchemist—'Simia' or 'Kimiyasaaz'. He directed his disciples to look for gold and silver in specific places—and they found the exact amount that he had specified, right there. The locals could not fathom the reason behind his prosperity. It was attributed

---

[50]Ibid., p. 129.

to various things like God's grace, mysticism, alchemy, and even sorcery.

The easy-going vibes of Jalaluddin's reign made the Sidi's khanqah a club of disgruntled nobility who often received financial help from him. Brinjtan and Hathia Payak were recipients of a stipend of one lac Jitals in Balban's reign, but were snubbed by the new Sultan. It was reported that they, together with one Qazi Jalaluddin Kashani and the Sidi, were planning a coup. It was alleged that Brinjtan and Payak were fidais (soldiers on suicide mission the term was originally used to designate heretics) and had plotted to sever the Sultan's head in the mosque during Friday's congregational prayers. It was also alleged that the Sidi, boosted by wealth and popularity, planned to usurp the throne. Thus, on the basis of such intelligence reports, the Sidi and his companions were arrested. Brinjtan and Payak were killed. Qazi Jalaluddin Kashani was sent to Badaon, and many of the Balbani and Muizzi bandagaan who frequented his khanqah were banished.

The Sidi was brought to Baharpur on the outskirts of the city. The Sultan wished to test his miraculous powers, claims to piety and his supposed Sayyid lineage (someone who is connected to the Prophet's bloodline). It would be a test of fire, owing to the Islamic belief that Ibrahim came out unscathed from the fire prepared for him by Nimrud, thus creating the popular notion that fire would not harm pious people of his bloodline. Thus the Sidi was to be thrown into a blazing pit. The Ulema (theologians/scholars) were dumbstruck, because fire was typically associated with hell and therefore its retributary use was supposed to be the exclusive prerogative of the Creator of fire. Fearing divine wrath for their silence in favour of worldly gains, some of them gathered courage and represented to the Sultan that fire's nature is to burn, and putting it to use in the day and age to test someone's innocence would be completely un-Islamic. Thus the Sultan desisted from putting the Sidi through the fire ordeal. However, he interrogated him personally. He was brought before the Sultan, bound in heavy chains and treated with contempt that he had never known. Although all his answers were logical and indicative of his righteousness, the Sultan was not convinced. Except for the testimony of a single man, there was no evidence against him. Nevertheless, blinded by insecurities, the Sultan ordered Abu Bakr Tusi Haidari—the chief of a Qalandar sect and a rival of the Sidi—to kill him. The Qalandars pounced on him and made cuts on his body with razors and knives and stabbed him hundreds of times with sack-makers' needles.[51] After unspeakable tortures, Arkali Khan ordered that his head be crushed under an elephant's foot.

As the Sufi's mangled body splurted blood, it stirred a raging storm that night. Dark clouds covered every star and the winds seemed to challenge human conceit. It didn't rain that year. Screams emanated from fissured and cracked lands, but skies watched in vengeful quietude. Crops failed. Families jumped into the Yamuna to save themselves of slow death by hunger, and became food for the alligators. It seemed that the royal treasury would soon be depleted. In

---

[51]*Muntakhab-ut Tawarikh*, p. 235.

the year following the dry spell, the skies unleashed such a ceaseless discharge that people recalled its terror for many years. The populace was in a bad mood, and they blamed Jalaluddin's injustice towards Sidi for this natural calamity. It was circulated that the Sufi had a premonition of his death, and used to sing the following verses days before it:

'In the kitchen of love, they slay naught but the good;
The weak natured and the evil they kill not.
If thou art a sincere lover, flee not from slaughter.
He whom they slay not is no better than a corpse.'[52]

In Kara, Alauddin applied all his diligence to accumulate wealth through military exploits. The booty collected from his initial success was offered to the Sultan. The latter, impressed by his industrious nephew and son-in-law, added Awadh to the former's iqta. Further, the central treasury's share from the taxes of these provinces was waived so that Alauddin could recruit additional forces and rake in money by raiding more territories. Although it was agreed that the first target of these raids would be Chanderi, he went farther to Deogir and amassed immense riches. Intelligencers' reports were laden with news of Alauddin's victories and wealth, and the in-house gossip indicated that the days of the princess' marriage with her zealous cousin were over. Since the Sultan was in Gwalior when clear intelligence reports of Alauddin's itinerary surfaced, his options were to move towards the victorious army and grab its spoils, or to wait where he

---

[52]Ibid.

was and order Alauddin to come to him, or to go back to Dilli and let Alauddin reach Kara and then chart a course of action in accordance with the latter's attitude towards his responsibilities to the centre. Ahmad Chap opined that treasure and sedition were inseparable and therefore the Sultan should take immediate charge of all the spoils. His advice reeked of distrust towards Alauddin and the trustful Sultan loathed this. The nobles, who were good at psychological manipulation, said what the Sultan wanted to hear—that Alauddin had been brought up by him as a son and therefore it was foolish to doubt his loyalty. Therefore, the Sultan should go back to the capital and wait for communication from his nephew. Even though Ahmad Chap had apprised the Sultan of the increasing frailty of his daughter's marriage, the latter refused to see any sense and let Alauddin go back to his stronghold.

Cunning diplomacy prompted Alauddin to hurry in sending an apology to the Sultan. He expressed his regret at leading an expedition without royal approval or information. He begged for a farman (royal order) promising amnesty, so that he could show his unfortunate face to the magnanimous Sultan and surrender himself and his possessions at his blessed feet. Men of even average political sagacity guessed that the apology had been sent as part of an elaborate hoax. Alauddin was buying time to organize an army and flee to Lakhnauti. However, Jalaluddin, who was a veteran of diplomatic and military expertise, couldn't see through the plan of a man trained by him. He waited on Alauddin hand and foot, and wrote the covenant as requested. The most trusted messengers were dispatched post-haste to Kara. They were supposed to assure the poor nephew of his uncle's affection for him, but on their arrival they witnessed, with shock and horror, military preparations. They tried their best to warn the Sultan, but failed. They were put under arrest. Alauddin had initially planned to establish his kingdom at Lakhnauti, but his unsuspecting uncle's doting letter encouraged him to stay put. Thus, according to a fresh design, his brother Almas Beg presented a false and conspiratorial letter before the Sultan, in which Alauddin had apparently written to Almas that he was so terrified of the Sultan's wrath, he carried poison in his turban. He pondered whether he should go into hiding or drown himself with all his treasures, or whether he should distribute his possessions and then commit suicide. According to the letter, Alauddin had said that he would survive his paranoia only if the Sultan went to Kara, held his hand and took him to Dilli under the shadow of his clemency. In the light of this communication, Jalaluddin jumped through hoops to shield his treacherous nephew—or maybe he was simply bothered by the thought of losing the treasures which he foolishly hoped would come to him.

It was Ramzaan (the Islamic month of fasting) and rains had set in. Movement of armies was usually avoided at such times, but an exception was made. Almas Beg was ordered to go post-haste to Kara to announce the Sultan's arrival so that Alauddin may be stopped from committing suicide or destroying the treasures. Sensing Alauddin's bait-and-switch strategy, the nobility tried to dissuade the Sultan but he was glued to his unreasonable programme.

Ahmad Chap was directed to travel by the land route and the Sultan, accompanied by approximately a thousand soldiers, travelled by road and river boats. Now Alauddin went about his preparations to usurp the sultanate with brazen assurance. When the sighting of the Sultan's boats was reported he sent Almas Beg into the waters, to request the Sultan to come ashore with a small body of disarmed men—because the sight of his majestic soldiers might terrorize Almas's docile brother to death. The Sultan's agreement to this shocking request petrified his officers. Two small boats were launched, and he embarked for the shore with a few unarmed men.

They were dumbfounded at the glimpse of the military paraphernalia that awaited them. Almas Beg explained that the army was in readiness to welcome the Sultan. The unsuspecting uncle believed him, but was hurt that Alauddin had absented himself from the banks; as per protocol he should have personally received the Sultan. Almas Beg clarified that he was busy supervising the preparations of Iftaar (the dusk meal with which Muslims break their fast) for their dearest uncle. This convinced the Sultan, but the others started reciting the 'Surah Yasin' (a chapter of the Quran usually read near a dying person) and prayed for forgiveness for their sins.

Finally, when Alauddin showed up and fell at the Sultan's feet, Jalaluddin immediately held him up with affection, kissed his eyes and cheeks and slapped him lovingly. Addressing him by his pet name Ali, he reassured him that even if the whole world turned against his beloved nephew, the Sultan wouldn't. For him, he would remain a little baby who wetted his lap, and the memories of those days were so fresh that it seemed that the smell of his urine hadn't faded yet. He assured Alauddin that no one was powerful enough to break the bond of their love and drew Alauddin close into a warm embrace.

This was the cue for the assassins. The first strike of the sword by Mahmud Salim didn't kill the Sultan, but wounded him grievously. He scrambled towards the boat, cursing his treacherous nephew; 'Wicked Ali, what did you do, what did you do?'[53] Then came the second blow, and neatly swept his head off his shoulders. All the men who had accompanied on the boat were also slain. Alauddin's hands were red with his affectionate uncle's blood. The head that wore the crown moments ago was fixed on a lance and exhibited right through Kara-Manikpur and Awadh. That exhibition simultaneously displayed Alauddin's victory and defeat. The vanquisher of the Sultan had been vanquished by Satan.

Oblivious to the losses involved in selling one's soul to the devil, he unwinded in the shade of the royal umbrella. In a couple of years, he eliminated all the nobles who had betrayed Jalaluddin to become partisans of his cause, because their unreliability was established beyond doubt. Salim, who had launched the offensive on the credulously affectionate Sultan, had to suffer in another way. His son contracted leprosy and no money given by Alauddin could stop the child's body from rotting—he simply disintegrated limb by limb as his father watched in

---

[53]*Tarikh-i Firoz Shahi*, p. 144.

helpless desperation. Ikhtiyaruddin Hud, who had artfully relieved the Sultan's body of its head, became insane. He hallucinated that Jalaluddin had come with a sword to cut off his head. Thus his delusions of grandeur were cured by horrific hallucinations. Alauddin had initiated his reign by destroying those who were close to him, and he was destined to end it by destroying those who were closer.

Ahmad Chap, who was supposed to join Jalaluddin at Kara, hurried back to Kilukheri at breakneck speed. Arkali Khan, the late Sultan's heir, was at Multan. In a situation which already seemed iffy, waiting for Arkali was hazardous and therefore his younger brother, Qadr Khan, was crowned as Sultan Ruknuddin Ibrahim. His mother, Malika-i Jahan, became the de facto ruler. They moved out of Kilukheri to the Red Palace in Dilli. Iqtas and offices were distributed amongst the Jalali bandagaan. On the other hand, Alauddin had started his journey from Iqtadar to Sultan. Some of the Jalali nobles thought it politic to support him voluntarily, and many others received kickbacks to fall in line. Barani reports that the bribe-prone were offered thirty to fifty mans of gold each. As the number of deserters from the nobility rose, Malika-i Jahan requested Arkali to come to Dilli to save the sultanate. She explained that Qadr Khan had been crowned only as a stop gap arrangement. Barani presents her communication as follows:

> I committed a grave mistake that in your presence when I put my younger son on the throne. Now none of the *maliks* and *amirs* pay heed to him and most *maliks* had joined Sultan Alauddin and the kingship is

slipping from our hands. If you can do it come post haste to us and occupy the throne of your father. Come for our assistance. This brother of yours who is sitting on the throne, you are his elder brother and you are most worthy and best suited for the kingship; he would stand before you and serve you. I am but a woman and women are deficient in judgement. I committed a mistake don't hold it against your mother. Take possession of your father's kingdom. In case if you persist in your anger and do not come, the way Sultan Alauddin is coming with might and glory, if he takes over Delhi, he would spare neither you nor us.[54]

Although Arkali could have matched Alauddin's military skills, the latter was all but assured of the crown due to the treacherous nobility. Therefore Arkali ignored Malika's pleading.

As a playmaker, Alauddin wanted to cover every bit of the political field. Thus gold and silver coins were scattered through 'manjaniqs' (artificial canons) for the commoners. Up to five mans of gold was shot every day. Thus the materially inclined rushed head over heels to offer their services to him, and the number of his soldiers multiplied overnight. Ibrahim was incapable of arresting Alauddin's domination, and thus he fled with whatever treasures he could carry. Accompanied by Malika-i Jahan and Ahmad Chap, he sought asylum with Arkali Khan.

On his arrival Alauddin camped at Siri. The initial uprising against Jalaluddin had borne witness to the power

---

[54]Ibid., p. 150.

of public opinion in the capital. So money, wine, sherbets and paan were freely distributed to pacify the common man. The manjaniqs spat precious coins on the roads and the citizens were swept off their feet. This apparent generosity was, in fact, a well calculated investment. Alauddin weighed that if he lost in the struggle for power at this stage, he would definitely be killed. Thus it was worth spending every tanka towards securing the crown. Secondly, if he became the Sultan, he would easily recover the principal, with compound interest.

His policy was a political expedient. Greed was carefully played up and conscience buried deep. The Jalali nobles were given the impression that the sultanate would be run in partnership with them. Ulugh Khan and Zafar Khan were sent to Multan to take down Jalaluddin's sons. Shaikhul-ul Islam, a cleric, mediated on their behalf. They surrendered before Ulugh Khan, who granted them asylum. A 'fatehnama' (declaration of victory) advertising the defeat of the rightful heirs was widely publicized. However, Alauddin was not done with them, not yet. They, together with Alghu Khan (a son-in-law of Jalaluddin) and Ahmad Chap, were blinded and imprisoned at Hansi, and all sons of Arkali Khan were killed. All the women of their harem, including Malika-i Jahan, were brought to Dilli. Thereafter Alauddin cracked the whip on the nobles who had deceived Jalaluddin. They were stripped of their titles and iqtas and their wealth was confiscated. They were blinded and imprisoned. They had finally deciphered Alauddin's cryptic largesse, but it was too late. Interestingly, those who had remained loyal to the late Sultan were spared.

Blessings seemed to cover every aspect of Alauddin's life. He vanquished enemies and won battles; his coffers overflowed with uncountable treasures; and his sons' laughter resounded through the harem. Puffed up with conceit, he called himself Sikandar-i Sani (Alexander-II) and even contemplated launching a new religion. One wonders whether Alauddin knew that his ideal of majesty, Alexander the Great, had realized at a rather young age that life extended beyond the purchasing power of money. Together with many other deceptively simple desires, spending some time with his family remained an unfulfilled wish of the dying world conqueror.

In-house rebellions, like that of Alauddin's nephews, were quashed with merciless resolve. Their eyes were gouged out with knives and they were beheaded. In the wake of one rebellion, all the sons and grandsons of Malik-ul-Umra Kotwal Fakhruddin were massacred. In 1290, the same Kotwal had traded in Kai Kaus' life for the life of his sons.

Money was identified as the motive power of sedition and therefore corrective measures were initiated. Almost overnight, the nobility was denuded of riches. Grants of all kinds—lands, land-revenue, gifts, honourariums, pensions and even religions endowments—were reviewed and most were revoked. People were scared to show off any wealth. Use of non-verbal signals came into vogue to escape the dense and opaque spy network. Social gatherings, especially of the influential families, were banned. Breweries were shut down and those who were addicted to intoxicants brewed them in their own homes at a great risk. Deep wells were dug to serve as prisons for defaulters. One of his decrees prescribed that if someone violated another's wife, the man would be castrated and the woman would be killed if she was adulterous. Prisoners were never released and exiles were never allowed to return.

The only place where gatherings continued—and the Sultan was unable to stop them—was the khanqah of Shaikh Nizamuddin Auliya. The doors to his khanqah were open for everyone, and so much food was served that guests ended up full and had to take some home. Jamal Qiwam reports that on the Sultan's orders, a spy came to the khanqah and sat at the place where food was being served. Khwaja Imam Pahelvi, who was sitting next to Shaikh Nizamuddin, whispered in his ears that the man in the front row was an informer of the Sultan. The Shaikh calmly said that the only thing that this fellow could report was that he saw them having a meal of meat and bread. Unconcerned with the presence of spies and reporters, he continued supervising the distribution of 'tehri' (a preparation of rice mixed with meat or vegetables) and 'sambosas' (a stuffed and deep fried savoury dish introduced by the Turks) amongst the needy.[55] To gauge the Sufi's inclination towards politics, the Sultan wrote a letter to him, that since the sufi was very popular amongst the people, who brought their problems to him for guidance and blessings, he understood the issues of the subjects at the grass-roots level—therefore if he informed the Sultan about the concerns of the people and directed him in administrative matters, the condition of the

---

[55] *The War that Wasn't*, pp. 170–71.

common man would improve. He also promised that his suggestions would be implemented forthwith. However, the Shaikh replied that a dervish has nothing to do with the Sultanate. This relieved the suspicious Sultan. Some sources report that he had expressed a desire to meet the Shaikh, but the latter politely declined the proposal, saying that he was praying for the Sultan in any case. On another occasion, he is reported to have said that he has two doors in his house—and if the Sultan enters by one, he would leave by the other. His predecessor Jalaluddin had also expressed such a desire, and when he wasn't granted time for an interview, he decided to go unannounced to the khanqah. However, Amir Khusrau, whom he had taken into confidence, informed his Pir about the plan. Therefore the Shaikh immediately left for Ajodhan to avoid the Sultan. When Jalaluddin came to know of Amir Khusrau's role in the matter, he was very angry but eventually forgave him. Although the Shaikh had been offered lands and orchards by both Jalaluddin and Alauddin, he never accepted such gifts from anyone.[56]

One of the most remarkable reforms introduced by Alauddin was in the economic sector. He introduced the concept of market control. Expert brokers were employed to assess the cost price of various commodities and their values were fixed accordingly. The prices of things as mundane as earthen bottles, combs and needles were also fixed. Merchandise could be bought from assorted bazaars and superintendents were employed to oversee the

---

[56] *Tarikh-i Firoz Shahi*, pp. 210–14 and *The War that Wasn't*, pp. 162–69.

transactions. The punishments for cheating customers were exemplary and Yaqub Nasir, the Diwan-i-Riyasat (finance minister), was a dreaded man. Nothing was undervalued or overvalued. Weights and measures were regularly inspected. If a vendor cheated on the quantity to be delivered, the difference was met by cutting off the same amount of flesh from his body. Permits were required to buy expensive cloth. This helped the government in keeping tabs on the rich. The salary of a cavalry man was fixed at 234 tankas and an additional 78 tankas were given for an extra horse. Cost of food items like wheat, rice, sugar and butter etc. were fixed, and the governors of the hinterlands were instructed to collect taxes in kind from some areas so that the state granaries were equipped to maintain fixed prices even in times of scarcity. No one dared to hoard or sell anything on the black market. The accounts of the revenue officials were rigorously audited and the penalty for discrepancies or corruption was death. Their job was so dire that no one wanted to marry their daughters to them.

The unruly zamindars were tamed and mounds were made out of the heads of the Mongols who threatened the glorious sultanate.[57] It was a wonder for the people of the times that an ill-tempered, ill-natured and hard-hearted man like Alauddin flourished as he did. Sycophants attributed Alauddin's well-rounded attainments to his 'karaamat' (miracles) and 'kashf' (mystical inspiration). However, in Alauddin's context, Barani strongly accredited it to 'istidraj' and 'makr' (fraud). According to him, if

---

[57] *Tarikh-i Firoz Shahi*, pp. 186–98.

anyone's miraculous or mystical powers were at work for the economic stability of the times, they were those of Shaikh Nizamuddin Auliya.[58] Alauddin's sons, Khizr Khan and Shadi Khan, had also become his disciples. It is reported that when the princes requested the Shaikh to induct them as his pupils, he warned them that they were used to the shade of the royal umbrella over their head, and his company would mean giving up those comforts for poverty, hardship, piety and self-control. However, the princes insisted and with their father's approval, became the Shaikh's disciples. To commemorate the occasion, they hosted a grand feast, complete with a 'sama' (a mystical musical), at the Shaikh's khanqah at Ghiyaspur (now Nizamuddin in New Delhi). It was a party for both saints and commoners. The brothers personally served the guests. Their very first lesson in humility, on the Shaikh's instructions, was to help the guests wash their hands. The people who had gathered there were impressed to witness a rare sight—the shahzaadas, amirs and maliks were serving the faqirs.[59]

While his sons were fortunate enough to learn a few lessons in humility, Alauddin's arrogance and anger increased with his ascendancy. He started believing that he could never make a mistake. Of course, he could not have been more mistaken. In fact, his blunder was not even new—he repeated the slip-up of his uncle Jalaluddin by trusting the wrong man. For Jalaluddin, he was that man,

---

[58]Ibid., pp. 145, 199, 207, 226 &233.
[59]*The War that Wasn't*, pp.135–36.

and for him it was Malik Kafur 'Hazaardinari'—a eunuch worth a thousand dinars.

Malik Kafur was an efficient and brave commander. He led many successful campaigns in the Deccan and South India (1309–1311). Over a period of time, Alauddin's admiration for him turned into an enigmatic passion. The officer went from strength to strength and became the Malik Naib-Wazir and Arz-i-Mamalik (prime minister and commander-in-chief of the Army). His ambitions were proportional to the Sultan's obsession with him. On the other hand, the heir Khizr Khan was more of a romantic dreamer than a zealous supremo. Success on the battlefield was often a good litmus test for an heirs' political preparedness. However, not only was he unprepared, he was also unaware that aspiration for the crown is generally accompanied by life-threatening hazards. To make matters worse, the Sultan's wrathful and irritable temperament pushed his family away from him. He faced the paradox of having enormous wealth in treasures but a depleted stock of humanity. Personal bonds splintered in the din of silver and gold tankas. Princes and ladies of the harem were too busy with social engagements and parties to register the gaping and growing distance between themselves and the Sultan. However, two astute people noticed it. One was Alp Khan, Khizr Khan's father-in-law, and the other was the Sultan's beloved Malik Kafur. The former wanted to fill the chasm between the Sultan and his family, and the latter tried to widen it. In this situation, Alauddin was struck down by Dropsy. An excess of watery fluid collected in the cavities and tissues of his body and introduced him to the frailty of the human form. For someone who was used to being in control, it was quite a shock. Far removed from realms of fantasy that he was used to, he became too weak to face up to his failing body. The discerning Malik Kafur used psychological tactics to exploit his insecurities and thus eliminate contenders. Alp Khan was assassinated and Khizr Khan was sent to Gwalior and imprisoned there. His mother, Bibi Mahak, was confined to the Red Palace. By this time, the Sultan was bedridden. He was ill and lonely, possibly cognizant of his misjudgements but incapable of undoing any of them. One morning, the news hounds reported that the Sultan was dead, and amidst rumours of his being poisoned by Malik Kafur, a six-year-old prince was raised to the throne under the title of Sultan Malik Shahabuddin Khalji.

Malik Kafur became the de facto ruler. The starting point of his privileges was the Sultan's infatuation with him, and the thrilling climax to this game came with the destruction of his lover by his own hands. Though he was a veteran of politics, he had not built a cadre of personal loyalists. His assumption that the Alai bandagaan would automatically accept him as their master was a huge miscalculation. His sword began to lose its cutting edge due to his blunt diplomatic skills. Rulers generally realize that it is incumbent on them to display generosity and amnesty—at least at the onset of their reign—but Kafur paraded his pettiness. Khizr Khan was blinded at Gwalior and Kafur ordered his barber to slice Shadi Khan's eyeballs out of their sockets like melons.[60] It is reported that when someone taunted the princes about the ineffectiveness of their discipleship with Shaikh Nizamuddin Auliya, they confidently replied that although their eyesight was being taken away, the visions of their hearts had been enhanced by the Sufi's blessings. They were hopeful that on Qayamat (the Day of Judgement), they would be safe under the shade of their Pir's banner.[61] Their mother, who had spent years as an affluent hostess of opulent jollities, was robbed to the last penny, humiliated and pauperized.

Alauddin's personal bodyguards, the Payaks, were shocked at this massive political haemorrhage. The rapid torment and elimination of the residents of the Hazaar Sutun palace jolted their self respect out of inaction. They were responsible for the protection of Alauddin's family, and were motivated to go down in History as brave loyalists. Thus, they vowed to avenge the dehumanization of their master's family. Unaware of the resentment brewing against him, Kafur was busy playing games with other eunuchs. He had set up a pavilion called Khurramgah as an interim court, from where orders were being issued to the nobles. Unable to withstand all this, one night, after locking the palace gates, the Payaks swiftly entered Kafur's bedroom and severed his head. This was merely the fifth day after Alauddin's death. They freed Qutbuddin Mubarak Khan, the eighteen-year-old son of Alauddin who had been imprisoned by Malik Kafur, and appointed him

---

[60] *Tarikh-i Firoz Shahi*, p. 230.
[61] *The War that Wasn't*, p. 189.

as the Naib of his brother Sultan Shahabuddin. However, his deputyship was essentially kingship and in a matter of two months he dispatched his young brother to Gwalior and had him blinded. Now the reign of Sultan Qutbuddin Mubarak Shah Khalji began.

Qutbuddin felt assured that his luck was shining, but in fact it was laughing and the joke was on him. His accession was seen by the Payaks as their victory. The bragging blabbermouths claimed that they were kingmakers and therefore demanded preferential treatment from the Sultan. The latter was tethered to systems of hierarchy and therefore could not do much to please his benefactors. Stressed by the cacophonies of their loud demands, he decided to silence them forever. Their unity was compromised and they were treacherously killed in suburban areas. Barani reports that the wise men who witnessed these brutal killings said:

'Oh you who have been killed, whom did you kill that you have been killed?

Now the one who killed you, when is he going to be killed?'[62]

The stifling rules of Alauddin's times were relaxed. Prisoners were released, land grants were increased and there was ease all around. Spy holes were closed and spymasters became jobless. People could talk and act freely. Tankas jingled in pockets and purses and the prices of commodities rose. The ban on intoxicants became a joke. Drunken men roamed the streets and indulged in every

---

[62]*Tarikh-i Firoz Shahi*, p. 232.

vice that intoxicants could promote. Attractive nautch girls, eunuchs and handsome slaves hiked up their rates and the prices of all luxury items shot skywards. Due to the Sultan's personal inclination, an orientation—homosexuality—which was, in those times, considered particularly immoral and evil, ran amok with saucy openness. He was smitten with a young man of the Barwar stock of Gujarat, called Hasan. Flooded with favours and privileges, Hasan was entitled Khusrau Khan and made the wazir of the Sultanate. Even momentary separation from the boy made the obsessed Sultan restless. On the other hand, Khusrau Khan found the Sultan unsexy. The latter's endless physical intimacy repulsed him and he felt like cutting his snake-hipped lover to pieces. However, he put up with the sexploitation patiently and waited for the right time to strike.

Unaware of the cobra pit he was nurturing under his pillow, the Sultan went about destroying random and remote portents of death. He ordered the assassination of his blind brothers, Khizr Khan, Shadi Khan and Malik Shahabuddin. Reportedly, when the princes were taunted that their reverence for Shaikh Nizamuddin could not reverse misfortune, they retorted that, in fact, they were blessed to be spared involvement in sordid worldly gains. Had they become rulers they would surely have shed the blood of innocent people and usurped the properties of orphans, and these sins are the fuel for hellfire.[63]

Malik Asaduddin, a son of Alauddin Khalji's uncle

---

[63] *The War that Wasn't*, pp. 188–89.

Yoghrish Khan, revolted. The uprising failed and besides Asaduddin, twenty-nine sons of Yoghrish were butchered. Most of them were young children. His wealth was confiscated and the women of his family were reduced to destitution. Nothing was done to hide or excuse the Sultan's cruelty. Zafar Khan, the Governor of Gujarat, and Malik Shahin, the Sultan's father-in-law, were also killed for insignificant reasons.

Khusrau Khan's maternal cousin Husamuddin was assigned the governorship of Gujarat. It was rumoured that the Sultan had sexual liaisons with him as well. Husamuddin attempted a coup in Gujarat which was subdued by the Alai loyalists, and he was dispatched back to Dilli. To the surprise of all the courtiers, the Sultan, who had ordered the culling of twenty-nine innocent children of Yoghrish Khan like animals, let off Husamuddin with just a mild slap. When Yak Lakhi Khan had revolted in Deogir, the same Sultan had ordered the amputation of his ears and nose and his subjection to public ridicule. All his supporters had been hunted and killed.

Perhaps the Sultan did not know that exceeding limits sets off a chain of pushbacks. Encouraged by the Sultan's leniency towards Husamuddin, Khusrau Khan became openly seditious. While leading an expeditionary force in Mabar, he confiscated great wealth from a particularly rich merchant and began planning a rebellion. Alai nobles Malik Tamar and Malik Taligha got wind of the plot he was hatching. They admonished him and dispatched him to the capital after alerting the Sultan. Much care was taken to ensure that he did not escape en route. The Sultan was also very eager to receive him, but unfortunately for different reasons. It was probably the first time in the History of the sultanate that royal palanquins were ferrying a seditious rebel from the capital's suburbs. In fact, there was a ready supply of strong palanquin bearers to reduce travelling time. The Sultan, oblivious to the impending doom, continued down his primrose path and Khusrau Khan's attractive body took priority over his seditious mind. Instead of imprisoning him for his disloyalty, the Sultan locked him in a lustful embrace. Now the foxy Wazir complained about the loyal nobles who had arrested him. Despite the testimony of senior officers and other crucial witnesses, the Sultan believed that Khusrau Khan was innocent and all evidence presented to him were but flimsy fabrications born out of jealousy. The accusers were punished in different ways. Thereafter, people realized that the anti-choice Sultan's love had made Khusrau Khan invincible, and no further reports against him surfaced.

The muted courtiers watched the acts of the royal clique in disgust. Sometimes the Sultan held the court in women's attire, loaded with jewels and gold and decked up in feminine make-up. At times one of his ill-bred 'bhands' (buffoons) came into the court touting his male organ and urinated on the clothes of the nobles; at other times he arrived totally naked and blabbered gross obscenities. Women of the harem passed vulgar comments at senior nobles in such high-pitched voices that all inmates of the Hazaar Sutun palace could hear them. The officials bore this embarrassment in silence, while the Sultan and his companions giggled and laughed hysterically.⁶⁴ Qutbuddin had the audacity to mock even Shaikh Nizamuddin Auliya, and it is believed that he had promised a prize of one thousand gold tankas for the Sufi's head. The inmates of the royal harem and nobles were not allowed to go to the Shaikh's khanqah. It is reported that a noble, Talbegha Boghdah, was a disciple of the Shaikh, and the latter had presented cap to him. Once, when he wore it in Qutbuddin's presence, the latter asked him to take it off. Even after being asked thrice, the noble refused to remove it. Thus the enraged Sultan drew his sword and threatened to cut off the defiant fellow's head. Boghdah immediately brought his head under the sword and said that he would rather die than dishonour his Pir's gift.⁶⁵ Fortunately the Sultan was more impressed than agitated, and he sheathed his sword, saying that this was what exemplary loyalty was and this was how loyal his companions should be to him.

An occasion for a more direct conflict with the Shaikh appeared when the Sufi overlooked the Sultan's orders to come and offer Friday's congregational prayer in a new mosque which he had constructed at Siri. The argument was that the mosque near his khanqah had more rights over his person and thus he would not abandon it for the sake of obeying a royal order.⁶⁶ Barani reports that on the occasion of Siwum in the mausoleum of Shaikh Ziauddin Rumi, the paths of the Sufi and the Sultan crossed and

---

⁶⁴*Tarikh-i Firoz Shahi*, pp. 242–43.
⁶⁵*The War that Wasn't*, pp. 180–81.
⁶⁶Ibid., p. 174.

they came face to face. Although the Shaikh said 'salaam' (a traditional Muslim greeting) to the Sultan, the latter had the audacity to ignore the saint whom even his arrogant father revered.[67] It is further reported that, probably for reasons of self aggrandizement, the Sultan ordered that all the ulema, mashaikh and imams should attend his court on the first full moon of every month. When Nizamuddin Auliya didn't report, he sent him a threat, saying that the saint should either report voluntarily or else force would be used to bring him in. It is a popular belief that the Shaikh prayed for the safety of his honour and consequently the Sultan was assassinated before the following full moon.[68]

Finally, when Qutbuddin had isolated himself from every sensible man, Khusrau Khan humbly asked for his permission to invite his Barwar clansmen from Bahlwal and Gujarat to settle in the capital. Once this was granted, the next request was to allow them into the palace complex. Accordingly, comfortable residences were allotted to them. They were generously favoured with governmental assignments, money, servants, horses, jewels and robes etc. Interestingly, all these men were not Khusrau Khan's relatives—some of them were professional assassins. So they lived in the palace and mulled over ideas of killing their host. A hunting expedition was always an adventurous lure for the Sultan. He would go on hunts drunk, making merry and totally distracted. It was initially planned that he would be bumped off in the middle of a hunt in the jungle.

---

[67] *Tarikh-i Firoz Shahi*, p. 243.
[68] *The War that Wasn't*, pp. 86–7 and 174.

However, a reasonable number of soldiers accompanied the monarch on such excursions and the Barwars feared that if they were identified as the assassins, a military backlash against them was assured. Therefore, killing him when he was alone in a closed and personal space seemed like a much safer bet. Accordingly, Khusrau Khan procured the keys to the doors which led to the most impregnable parts of the palace—the harem and the Sultan's bedchamber. He claimed that although his affectionate relatives had left their homes to be with him, due to his professional and personal engagements, they were neglected. With the Sultan's permission, Khusrau would invite them over to his apartment whenever he was free at night so that he could spend some time with them. In a seduced and sedated state, the Sultan permitted this and became the warrantor of a horrifying security breach. Khusrau Khan got the required keys and some three or four hundred men assembled near his quarters each night. The palace guards were alarmed because these men were armed and their smug demeanour reeked of sedition. However, just as greed had blinded Jalaluddin Khalji, Qutbuddin Khalji was blinded by lust. Everyone saw that his assassins had arrived—everyone except him.

Qazi Ziauddin, the 'kulliddar' (in-charge of the keys of the palace) felt affection for the Sultan since the latter had been his pupil as a child. Thus he could not resist warning the Sultan about the clearly foreseeable catastrophe. Sounding as diplomatic as he could, he pleaded that the palace guards were suspicious of the motives of the Barwars, who had been granted access into the innermost portions of the palace. He reminded the Sultan that in this father's times, even drinking an extra sip of water led to a determined inquisition and thus the presence of armed men at odd hours was unusual enough to be probed. He insisted that it would be wise to err on the side of caution. If the suspicion was proven wrong, the guards would be freed of their anxieties and relax, and Khusrau Khan's prestige would be further enhanced. However, if their hunch turned out to be true, a great tragedy could be averted and the Sultan's life would be saved.

Unfortunately the Qazi was rebuffed in no uncertain terms, and while he was being scolded, Khusrau Khan walked in. The Sultan told him everything that the Qazi had stated. Needless to say, the devious Khusrau was grateful to his stars for the Sultan's stupidity. Murmuring thanks under his breath, he let out a wail, crying that everyone hated him because the monarch loved him. The Sultan instantly planted a kiss on his lips and said that peoples' opinions notwithstanding, his love would remain solid as a rock. To prove a point to the poor Qazi and pacify his lover at that very moment, Khusrau Khan was given the keys of the stores and treasure houses as well. The Sultan promised that anyone who tried to harm even a single strand of his beloved's hair would not be spared. The Qazi's head hung in shame. Worried and dejected, he left for his office on the ground floor and busied himself in preparing the guards' duty roster. When the first quarter of the night had passed and most people had left for the night, Khusrau Khan's relatives Randhol and Jaharia walked into the palace with some other Barwars. They headed for the Qazi's office and after salutations, offered him a paan. When the poor man was engaged in conversation, one of them suddenly cut off his head in a single stroke of the sword. Now the suspense had ended and panic began. Tackling this situation was the acid test of the palace guards' ability, but the Barwars outnumbered them by hundreds. Therefore, most of them ran and hid in whatever corner they could find.[69]

Hazaar Sutun trembled in anticipation of the horrors which were to follow. Conversely, unaware of the feverish bloodlust on the ground floor, the debauch Sultan enjoyed a light moment with his beloved. Nevertheless, when the sounds rose and were carried to him by the winds, he asked Khusrau Khan to check what was happening. The con man, being a good actor, went to the rooftop for some time and then reported that a few horses had strayed from the stables and were causing a commotion across the palace courtyard. In the meantime, Jaharia and some other Barwars reached the upper storey of the Hazaar Sutun. Ibrahim and Ishaq, who guarded the door to the Sultan's private chamber, were slain. On hearing their cries, the ghastliness of the situation dawned on Qutbuddin and he wobbled in a crazed manner towards the harem.

Khusrau Khan knew that if the Sultan managed to escape into the harem it might become difficult to kill him—so it was now or never. Therefore he ran behind him and grabbed his shining tresses, coiling them around his wrist in an unyielding grip. A scuffle followed on the ground and the Sultan managed to sit on Khusrau Khan's

---

[69] *Tarikh-i Firoz Shahi*, pp. 246–49.

chest and beat it, but the fellow still did not let go of his hair. Just then, Jaharia Barwar arrived and wounded the Sultan in the chest with his sword. He was lifted off Khusrau Khan's ribs by his mane, dashed to the ground and relieved of his head. The Barwars threw the headless body of the Sultan from the roof to the courtyard of the Hazaar Sutun—a literal downfall. Servants recognized his body and ran away in a bid to save their lives, and some of them joined the Barwars for the same reason. Torches were lit and the harem was raided. Barani writes that the Barwars, with stinking mouths and armpits, ran riot in the Sultan's harem.

Khusrau Khan took Qutbuddin's wife for himself. Farid Khan and Umar Khan, the youngest sons of Alauddin Khalji, were killed. Farid Khan's mother was also killed. The royal ladies were violated by the barbaric rustics. All the nobles who were known to be loyal to Qutbuddin were assassinated. Many of them were called to the palace and beheaded. Their blood coloured the corners and corridors of the palace. The ladies of their houses were dishonoured, and their wealth, of course, was looted. Members of Qazi Ziauddin's family had fled, but his entire establishment was given to Randhol, and Jaharia was decked up in jewels and pearls. Barani believed that Jalaluddin's soul, which had been restless due to Alauddin's betrayal, was finally relieved of agony that night. While sipping the nectar of divine justice, it enjoyed the violence from the roof of the Hazaar Sutun and inside the harem.[70] He writes:

---

[70]Ibid., p. 251.

'Whatever he (Alauddin) did to the women and children of others, others are doing the same to his wives and children and the barbarities that he perpetrated on others, others are perpetrating the same barbarities on his household. So that people should know that anyone who commits wrongs to others in fact he commits it up on himself and one who uproots someone else in reality uproots himself. This is an example for the people to see regarding the household of Sultan Alauddin in this world.'[71]

Khusrau Khan ascended the throne as Sultan Nasiruddin. A new chapter began—but not new enough to be delinked from the past.

---

[71]Ibid., p. 233.

Chapter IV

Humanness and Baadshah Humayun

Not every arm which contains strength
Breaks the hand of the weak for showing bravery
Injure not the heart of the helpless
For thou will succumb to the force of a strong man—
Abandon thy claim to strength and manliness
Thou art weak minded and base
Whether thou be a man or woman,
If thou art able, make a sweet mouth
Although able to tear up an elephant's front
He is not a man who possessed no humility
A man's nature is of Earth
If he is not humble, he is not a man.

—SAADI SHIRAZI, *The Golestan*[72]

---

[72]Saadi Shirazi, *The Golestan*, translation Richard Francis, Iran Chamber Society, p. 83.

Timeline: The sixteenth century

Backdrop: Nasiruddin Muhammad Humayun was the second Emperor of the Mughal dynasty of India. On the paternal side, the Mughals traced their descent from Timur, the Central Asian conqueror of the clan of Chaghatay. He was perhaps the last of the nomad chiefs to have established a political dominion of an imperial ranking. Matching this, their ancestry from the maternal side has been traced to the supremely successful—though not equally sophisticated—Mongol conqueror Chengiz Khan. The ontogenesis of the Mughal Empire lay in Zahiruddin Muhammad Babur's victory over the Afghan Sultan Ibrahim Lodi in the first battle of Panipat in April 1526. The initial resistance babur faced from Ibrahim was an advance party that the Sultan had sent to Punjab in February 1526. Babur sent his son Humayun with a section of the Mughal forces to tackle this confrontation. The seventeen-year-old prince was successful in completely routing the Afghans. In fact, he also managed to bring back prisoners of war, who were executed by shooting on Babur's orders. It was very unlike Babur to be unnecessarily cruel, but this was done to demoralize his opponents before the next engagement. Ibrahim died fighting on the battlefield and a new era was born. Humayun was quickly dispatched to Agra by his father to seize the treasures there. Time was an important factor, because a change of guards often entailed looting of palaces. So Humayun proceeded at a breakneck speed to take charge of the Lodi capital. In the fort, besides others, he found the family of Raja Vikramajit of Gwalior, who had fallen fighting bravely for Ibrahim's cause at Panipat. Humayun took the family under his protection, and to reciprocate his goodwill, they presented to him a matchless diamond—the Koh-i-Noor. The prince presented it to Babur on his arrival but the latter gave it back to him. Babur's casual estimation of its cost was that it could generate enough funds to buy two-and-a-half day's worth of provisions—for the entire world.

Born to Maham Begum, Babur's favourite wife, in March 1508, Humayun was a much loved prince. His mother was extremely protective about him, because she had lost all her other children. He was the heir apparent, which further added to her worries about his security. When he was posted at Badakshan at the young age of twelve, she also left Babur's harem to be with him. On her return, she sunk into gloom over separation from her child. To fill that void, she adopted two children of Dildar Begum, another wife of Babur. Her sway over him was impressive. When he was preoccupied with preparations for the battle of Bajour (1519), she sent him an urgent letter that was an advance petition for the future adoption of Dildar Begum's unborn child. The further demand she made of her extremely busy husband was to foretell the unborn child's sex through divination. Although Babur disapproved of such practices, he did the needful to pacify Maham. Accordingly, names signifying male and female genders were written on separate pieces of paper, which were then wrapped in soft clay and dried into tiny balls. They were then dropped in warm water. The ball which opened first supposedly foretold the sex of the child. Notwithstanding his immediate mission, which entailed terrible risks, Babur found time to send her the prediction that it would be a boy—and indeed, he was right. This boy was named Hindal, after Hindustan.[73] The other child adopted by Maham was a girl, Gulbadan Begum, the author of *Humayun Nama*. She writes that Maham was loved so much by Babur that when she came from Kabul to join him in Hindustan in 1527, he, at forty-five years of age, didn't wait for a horse to be saddled for him—he ran to receive her.[74]

Like his mother, Humayun also subscribed to interpretations of omens and charms. As a child, one morning, he decided to ask the names of the first three persons he met. He believed that the meanings of those names would indicate his future. The names turned out to mean 'desire', 'well-being', and 'triumph'.[75] Another time, he ordered that his pet white cockerel, which woke him every morning like an alarm clock, be brought to his tent since he had superstitiously assumed that if it sat on his shoulder, it would be an omen of good luck.[76] On yet another occasion, he had his own and the Persian monarch's names written on divinatory arrows and shot to prophesize the extent of their respective domains. Unfortunately, the Shah's spies at Humayun's court reported in Persia that Humayun had used arrows of an inferior quality for the Shah's name. The Persian monarch accosted Humayun on this matter when the latter

---

[73] Rummer Godden, *Gulbadan Portrait of a Rose Princess at the Mughal Court*, The Viking Press, New York, 1980, pp. 29–30.
[74] Ibid., p. 55.
[75] Ibid., p. 36.
[76] Ibid., pp. 83–4.

was a refugee in the former's empire. Although embarrassed, Humayun managed to handle the situation rather well.

As an emotional man, he seemed to be deeply attached to his family, and thus resented distant postings. However, he actively assisted his father in the foundation of the Mughal Empire and eventually succeeded him. His life is a story of ups and downs. His three brothers, Kamran, Askari and Hindal, covered quite a bit of his political field, and their loyalties shifted from time to time. Kamran and Askari were full brothers; therefore, they formed a reasonably steady team. Hindal had been brought up by Humayun's mother, and Hindal's mother also had a soft corner for Humayun. Although he had let Humayun down many times, eventually he died fighting on his side.

Humayun's reign was sliced into two halves because of the Sur interregnum. He succeeded Babur in 1530 and was ousted out by Sher Shah Suri in 1540 after being defeated in the battles of Chausa and Kannauj. Humayun fled to Persia under extremely testing circumstances, and returned to Hindustan in 1555 with the help of the Persian monarch, Shah Tahmasp.

Subverting the historical narratives that portray him as a mediocre ruler, this section celebrates his simplicity, which easily transcends sophistication.

Humility as Strategy, and the Recovery of Bahadur Shah's Treasure

In 1535, when Humayun was at war with Sultan Bahadur Shah of Gujarat, a long siege ensued and Bahadur Shah's supply line was cut off by the Mughals. As time passed, the situation became so grim that his soldiers had to resort to eating horseflesh for survival. Finally, when defeat seemed imminent, the Shah scarpered from Gujarat to Mandu, then to Champanyer, and finally to Cambay. As a standard practice, every useful item which couldn't be carried was either hidden or destroyed. For example, his guns—called Laila and Majnu—were destroyed by his own commander, Rumi Khan. However, intelligencers informed Humayun that a treasure was hidden at Champanyer. Yet, despite great efforts, it couldn't be located.

Incidentally, Alam Khan, an officer of Bahadur Shah, defected to Humayun's side. The latter's officers advised Humayun that Alam should be apprehended and tortured into revealing the location of the treasure. However, Humayun opined that having come across to the Mughal camp voluntarily, the fellow had displayed confidence in their worth, and therefore victimizing him would be immoral. Besides, as a principle, humiliation should not be employed where humility might work. Therefore, a banquet was thrown and Alam was served wine with the intent to surprise and mellow him. Finally, in an inebriated state, he revealed that the treasure was buried right under the pool over which they were seated. Immediately, men were employed to throw out buckets full of water to empty the pool. But Alam intervened and enthusiastically showed them a plughole through which the water was drained in an instant. The treasure thus retrieved was enough to fill the shields of each and every soldier in accordance with his rank. Later, a well full of silver and gold ingots was also tracked. Thus, force was avoided and friendship worked.[77]

A Baadshah's Word and Promises Unbroken

In the battle of Chausa (1539), when Sher Shah busted the Mughal army with a surprise attack, Humayun was completely nonplussed. Negotiations with Sher Shah had probably implied that their armies would not engage at that juncture. However, they did, and in the ensuing attack Humayun struck one of his opponent's elephants with such aggression that his spear got stuck in the poor creature's body, and while he was trying to retrieve it, an arrow brushed his arm. Enemies began surrounding him and his calls for assistance went unheard, since his personal defenders were absorbed in saving themselves from the raptorial Afghans. So he hastily withdrew from the battlefield and somehow reached the banks of the Ganges. The speedy currents of the water alerted his horse's instincts to turn away, but that was hardly an option. Caution at this moment was rather risky, and so the diffident animal was persuaded by his master into the torrent. The horse eventually drowned, but Humayun was saved by the innovative skills of a water carrier who filled his leather bags with air so that the Baadshah could be buoyed up to safety. Once ashore, he asked his saviour's name, which was Nizam. So the grateful monarch promised that he would seat Nizam on Humayun's own throne so that

---

[77]Jouher Aftabchi, *Tazkirat-ul Waqiat*, translation Major Charles Stewart, Idarah-i Adabiyat-i Delli, Delhi, 1972, pp. 5–6.

his name would become immortal like that of his namesake, the Sufi Shaikh Nizamuddin Auliya.[78]

When Nizam eventually presented himself, the royal family was in the middle of a not-so-happy reunion. All the sons of Babur had gathered to put their house in order. On Kamran's request, Humayun had quickly forgiven Hindal's rebellion and, in fact, he had gone to Dildar Begum with a copy of the Quran to pledge on it that he had no malice in his heart for her son. As he lifted the Quran to prove the veracity of his words, Dildar snatched it from him, implying that she believed him. On the same occasion, he shared his grief over the loss of his daughter Aqiqa in the battle of Chausa, and told Gulbadan that regret was consuming him for taking the little child and the other ladies of the harem along with them to the war zone. He was thankful that Gulbadan had not witnessed that terrifying battle.[79] Kamran was quite disgusted with the Baadshah's shameful defeat. The Mughal house was seriously worried over Sher Shah's untamable ambitions. Of course, their fears were not misplaced. In the middle of all this, Humayun was informed that Nizam had come to see him. His siblings, including the mild Gulbadan, were shocked to learn that he was actually going to keep the promise he had made in a moment of fervid gratefulness. And he did. The water carrier was not just physically seated on the throne for two days, but the actual power to endow and appoint

---

[78]*Gulbadan*, pp. 17–18.
[79]Ibid., pp. 78–80.

was delegated to him.[80] Further, nobles were made to pay respect to him. Kamran Mirza was livid, and in protest he wrote to his brother: 'Gifts and favors of some other kind ought to be the servant's reward. What propriety is there in setting him on the throne? At a time when Sher Khan is near, what kind of affair is this to engage your Majesty?'[81] According to him, such insistence in keeping a promise was ridiculous and extortionate. Perhaps extraordinary would have been a better word. The content of the vow made its actualization even more laudable. A material reward would certainly have been easier, but by seating a poor man on the throne, Humayun was setting a new standard of commitment. In fact, he had a thing for keeping his word. Although his brothers may have never realized it, he forgave their repeated treacheries because he felt bound by the promise he had made to their dying father.

In 1530, Babur had organized an excursion to Dholpur. This was to help the ladies of the harem in managing their grief over the death of two infant princes, Alwar and Farukh. While the royals were there, Humayun left his post at Badakshan in charge of a young Hindal. Although Babur wasn't particularly pleased with this initiative, he allowed him to proceed to Delhi. Before the posting in the north-west frontier could be restrategized, Humayun fell ill. The royal jaunt was curtailed and a distraught Maham reached her son's bedside. Her conversation with Babur in these circumstances is recorded as follows: 'Do not be

---

[80]*Tazkirat-ul Waqiat*, p. 19.
[81]*Gulbadan*, p. 80.

troubled about my son. You are a king; what griefs have you? You have other sons. I sorrow because I have only this one.' And Babur replied, 'Maham! Although I have other sons, I love none as I love your Humayun. I crave that this cherished child may have his heart's desire and live long, and I desire the kingdom for him and not for the others, because he has not his equal in distinction.'[82] Babur was doubly tortured by the sight of his careworn beloved and their comatose son. Disillusioned and disappointed with the ineffectiveness of medication, they turned to frantic prayers. It was contemplated that the Koh-i-Noor diamond should be given as 'sadqa' (almsgiving) for Humayun's life but that, Babur thought, would be too little. The sadqa had to be something bigger, better, unmatchable yet well-matched with his son—it had to be himself. Accordingly, he took supplicatory rounds of Humayun's bed, begging God for his son's life in exchange for his own. Perhaps his prayers were accepted, because the malady switched from Humayun to him. Babur became enfeebled as Humayun recovered.[83] Despite his hectic military career, Babur had always found time for his family—whether it was escorting his mother for a visit to her relatives or taking his wives and children for a picnic. His illness enshrouded the whole harem in gloom. His daughters Gulrang and Gulchihra were married off in great haste, since his concerns regarding them were typical of any ordinary parent. However, one of his wishes that remained unfulfilled was to meet his youngest son, Hindal.

---

[82]Ibid., 65–6.
[83]Ibid.

At his dying father's behest, Humayun promised that he would never quarrel with his brothers nor entertain any evil intentions towards them. This vow remained imprinted on his soul, and he desisted from imbruing his hands with their blood despite their recurrent duplicity.[84] Askari and Hindal had let him down on various occasions, and were repeatedly forgiven. However, it was Kamran who tested his patience the most.

Political compulsions were inclining Humayun towards centralization, and that probably fuelled the unending tension between the brothers. From 1545 to 1553, a lot of Humayun's efforts were directed only towards tackling Kamran's resistance. Once, after a violent battle, Humayun wrote him a warning saying that Kamran could not escape accountability for unnecessary bloodshed, but he received a defiant reply—that the bride called 'kingdom' belongs to the one who embraces her across the edge of a sharp sword.[85] Another time, when Kamran feigned friendship, Humayun welcomed him with open arms—but of course the act didn't last. When Humayun was pressing siege to take Kabul from Kamran (1546–47), the infant Akbar, who was in his uncle's custody, was exposed on the fort ramparts to stop Humayun from using gunpowder. Being forgiven for this as well, he again betrayed Humayun and the Baadshah was wounded so badly in the ensuing confrontation that he was feared dead (1549)—and Hindal actually died fighting Kamran's Afghan allies (1551). The

---

[84] *Tazkirat-ul Waqiat*, p. 26.
[85] Ibid., p. 91.

last straw was his endeavor to join Sher Shah's son Islam Shah in 1552. In 1554, when Kamran was finally arrested and brought to Humayun's chamber, the Baadshah seated him on the same bed as himself—Akbar on his left and Kamran on his right. They shared a watermelon. Dodging excessive pressure from associates for Kamran's execution, Humayun reluctantly ordered his blinding. The persons deputed for the job were in no hurry to carry it out, because they feared that if the Badshaah's heart softened after the task was executed they would be in an unnecessary mess. In fact, one of them ran after Humayun to get a reconfirmation of the order.[86]

In 1555, when Humayun secured his first victory over the Afghans on his way back to Hindustan, the occasion was marked by a jamboree. The Ghakkar chief, who was an ally of the Afghans, had been defeated at Firozpur. The enemies had been routed and many were imprisoned. When an order was issued for the presentation of all the prisoners of war before the Baadshah, an officer, Ferhad Khan, reminded him that he had pledged that if the war goes in his favour, no one would be imprisoned. Accordingly, a 'farman' (order issued by a monarch) for the release of all the captives was issued forthwith.[87] Clearly, Humayun wouldn't break a promise even if it meant getting his own heart or bones broken.

---

[86]Ibid., pp. 105–6.
[87]Ibid., 114.

Magic in Misery and the Madness of Love

Robbed of his empire, betrayed by those he trusted and a fugitive flying for his life—this was Humayun's state when he first saw Hamida Banu Begum and fell in love with her, literally at first sight. This happened at Patar-Sind in 1541 when he was being hosted by Hindal and his mother Dildar Begum. A feast had been organized in his honour and there he saw Hindal's preceptor Shaikh Ali Akbar's daughter Hamida. Apparently the young prince was also in love with her. Humayun's earlier marriages had been arranged by Maham, and it was for the first time that, at thirty-three years of age, he was truly smitten with a girl nineteen years younger than himself. Adding to the problems of his amorous state were Hindal's resistance and Hamida's reluctance to marry him. Hindal had the audacity to threaten Humayun that he would withdraw his support if the Baadshah did not give up the ridiculous idea of a love marriage in the middle of a political and military crisis. Hamida, on the other hand, said that she would rather marry a man whose lapel she could hold, than one whose pedestal she would never be able to reach. No one knows whether she was referring to Humayun's age or position, or was simply disappointed by his circumstances; nevertheless, there was some kind of hesitation.[88] Shireen Moosvi's translation of the *Humayun Nama* provides interesting details about the circumstances of this marriage:

---

[88]*Gulbadan*, pp. 84–6.

The women of the Mirza's (Hindal's) household and all his people attended on His Majesty (Humayun) at this visit. Seeing Hamida Banu Begum, he asked, 'Who is she?' My mother (Dildar Begum) replied, 'She is the daughter of Mir Baba Dost.' Khwaja Muazzam (Hamida's Banu's brother) was standing in front of His Majesty. She said of him, 'This boy is a relation of ours,' and of Hamida Banu Begum, she also remarked, 'She too is a relation of ours.'

In those days Hamida Banu Begum was often at the Mirza's camp. The next day His Majesty again came to meet my mother Dildar Begum. He said, 'Mir Baba Dost is our kinsman; it would be befitting if you betroth his daughter to me.' Mirza Hindal offered excuses, saying, 'I regard this girl in the same light as a sister or daughter. His majesty is the King; suppose he does not make adequate provision, so that there is some vexation later?' His majesty became angry, got up and left.

Afterwards my mother wrote a letter to His Majesty to the effect that the mother of the (betrothed) daughter always takes airs. It is strange that His Majesty took exception to such few words and left. In reply the King wrote, 'This explanation has been very pleasing to us. Whatever airs you assume, I will subject myself head and heart to them. As far as the provision (for the bride) is concerned, of which you have written, God willing, it shall be such as is wished. I await your response.' [...] The next day, His Majesty came to my mother and asked her to send someone to

Hamida Banu Begum to bring her. My mother sent for her, but she did not come and replied, 'If the intention is that I should attend on His Majesty, I have had that honour on that day. For what else should I come?' His Majesty thereupon sent Subhan Quli to Mirza Hindal and asked him to send the Begum. The Mirza said, 'Despite whatever I have said she does not go; you yourself should go to her and ask her.' Subhan Quli went and asked her. (Hamida Banu) Begum answered, 'For the kings to see (a woman) once is lawful, the next time she becomes a stranger, seeing whom is unlawful I will not come.' Subhan Quli who heard these words from the Begum conveyed these to His Majesty. His Majesty remarked. 'If she is a stranger (na-mahram), we will (marry her to) make her accessible (mahram).' Thus for forty days efforts and coaxing went on to persuade (Hamida Banu) Begum, but she would not consent. At last my mother, Dildar Begum, admonished her, 'After all, you will be given (in marriage) to someone; better it is the King who receives you.' The Begum retorted: 'Yes, but let me be given to someone whose collar my hand can reach, rather than that I be given to a man, whose skirt, as I know well, my hand will not reach.' The last time my mother admonished her greatly. So after forty days, in the month of Jumada I 948 (23 August–21 September 1541) at the place called Patar, on a Monday, at midday, which His Majesty determined by holding the astrolabe in his own hand, and choosing the auspicious hour, he called Mir Abu'l Baqa to perform the marriage rites.

He gave two lakh (tankas) to Mir Abu'l Baqa as the marriage fee.[89]

Although Humayun had many other problems to sulk about, living as he did in the here and now, scripting his love story became a priority. His feelings for Hamida were a mix of teenage flicker and mature smouldering. Luckily, Dildar Begum stepped up to negotiate. She convinced Hindal that it was his duty to honour the wishes of his elder brother. The prince was left with no choice but to agree, though in protest he immediately inclined towards the anti-Humayun camp. Eventually, after almost a month of persuasion, Hamida also conceded. Excited over this intervention of good luck in a general series of trials, Humayun himself worked out an auspicious date and the wedding was solemnized with Dildar's blessings. This would prove to be one of the best amongst Humayun's emotional investments.

After just three days of the marriage he resumed his journey. Hamida became a partner in the challenges that her husband faced. Her pregnancy in the midst of a journey laden with dangers definitely added to her burdens. In this state, when it was sometimes difficult to find something as basic as water, she had a craving for pomegranates. The possibility of finding one in the middle of a desert was almost non-existent, and Humayun was saddened by his inability to fulfil such a mundane wish of his beloved wife. Fortunately, the Mughal party chanced upon a

---

[89]Shireen Moosvi, *Episodes in the Life of Akbar*, National Book Trust, New Delhi, 1994, pp. 1–3.

merchant who had a single piece of the required fruit. It was immediately procured.⁹⁰ Humayun's happiness over this fluke could easily equal his dejection over losing his kingdom. His childlike enthusiasm reflected his spirit of living in the moment.

Despite the dangers involved in displeasing Humayun's Afghan antagonist—the powerful Sher Shah Suri—the ruler of Umarkot, Raja Rana Prasad, agreed to give him refuge and assistance. In the last lap of the journey towards his domains, a heavily pregnant Hamida rode a horse borrowed from an officer called Roshan Beg. However, due to the indisposition of the horse that Beg was riding, he demanded the one that he had lent. Humayun immediately alighted from his own and seated Hamida on that horse. Roshan's animal was gracefully returned and the Baadshah started walking on foot. After a tiresome walk he mounted a camel—not the ride preferred by royalty. Eventually, another officer, Khalid Beg, gave his horse to the Baadshah. The fact that an officer could demand his animal back from Hamida is a reflection of Humayun's approachability.⁹¹

While Humayun was away to mobilize military assistance, at Umarkot, Hamida gave birth to a male child. And so on 15 October 1542, Jalaluddin Muhammad Akbar, the greatest of the Great Mughals, was born. On receiving the good news, Humayun didn't postpone celebrations for another time—just as he hadn't postponed falling in love. He broke a pod of musk and distributed the fragrant

---

⁹⁰*Gulbadan*, p. 88.
⁹¹*Tazkirat-ul Waqiat*, pp. 42–3.

substance, hoping that his son's fame would spread like the musky scent.[92]

Hamida stood by her husband through all his trials. As a mother, she aided the assertions of sovereignty by Akbar. To cut Bairam Khan, his dominating 'wakil' (regent), down to size, she married Akbar to the former's rival Munim Khan's granddaughter—the daughter of Mirza Abdullah Mughal. The wakil was against this match for obvious reasons, but the queen celebrated the wedding with defiant pomp and show. After her arrival from Kabul, the nobility's confidence in Bairam Khan waned.

Defeat Isn't Necessary, Victory Is

In 1541–42, under threat from Mirza Shah Husain in Sindh, Humayun and his entourage were to cross a river in vessels made of cattle hide. The Baadshah and some officers were yet to cross and a single boat remained. The hot-headed Tardi Beg, one of his officers, insisted on preceding him. This agitated the superintendent, who felt that Tardi was flouting protocol. In the following showdown the officer hit him with his horsewhip and in the heat of the moment the superintendent also drew his sword. Humayun was informed, and instead of being angry with Tardi for trying to cross before him, he decided to guard his honour. The superintendent's hands were tied with a handkerchief, symbolizing handcuffs, and he was presented before the noble. Embarrassed by the Baadshah's magnanimity and

---

[92]Ibid., p. 45.

ashamed of his conduct, Tardi quickly untied the fellow, apologized for his conduct and gave him presents to seal the reconciliation. On another occasion, when the group was being pursued by Askari, Humayun's request to Tardi for a horse was turned down. Therefore, he had to seat Hamida on his own horse during that chase—but he never held a grudge.[93]

Jauhar informs that on the way to Persia, when the condition of the Baadshah and his entourage worsened everyday, nobles lost hope and started deserting him. The Baadshah wanted his supporters to hold on, because driven by his inexplicable optimism he believed that eventually everything would fall in place. At one point the situation hit such a low, that Humayun had to personally keep an eye on his officers. Jauhar narrates: 'In the morning the king being necessitated to go out of the tent, he said to Tardi Beg and Munim Khan, "Remain here till I return," but as soon as he went out they both ran towards their horses. On which one of the attendants informed his Majesty that the two chiefs were going. He desired the attendant to call them back; but as they paid no attention to the call, the King himself ran after them, and with great difficulty prevailed on them to return. After this unworthy attempt, the king ordered that Munim Khan should be confined and Tardi Beg being frightened consented to remain.'[94] As it turned out, these officers remained loyal to Humayun and thereafter to his son Akbar.

---

[93]Ibid., pp. 33, 41 & 52.
[94]Ibid., p. 35.

Balancing Authority with Affection: Jauhar and the Baadshah

Jauhar Aftabchi, the author of *Tazkirat-ul-Vaqiyat*, was a devoted servant of Humayun and his personal water-bearer. The *Tazkirat-ul-Vaqiyat* was compiled on Akbar's orders. It is the only eyewitness account of the trials that the Baadhshah and his followers faced between 1540 and 1555. Jauhar narrates that in the course of their journey, they once faced a terrifying scarcity of water, and people died of thirst. In these circumstances, the Baadshah's bottle of drinking water ran dry and so, on his command, Jauhar filled it with the water that he had in the ewer for ablutions etc. and gave it to the king. Now the servant was left with no water at all, and the thought of being separated from his master and dying of thirst scared him; so he poured some of the water back from the Baadshah's water bottle into his ewer. Humayun noticed this and with his typical equitableness, approved of the division.[95]

One morning, a deer emerged from the jungle near their encampment and, dodging many arrows, dashed towards a nearby lake. In these times of scarcity a hunt would have ensured at least one good meal. Jauhar was by the lake when Humayun, chasing the deer, instructed him to shout out to men on the other shore to drive the animal back to their side. The stressful swimming fatigued the poor creature and noticing this, Jauhar rushed into the current to catch it alive. Certain of success and doubly sure of his master's liberality, he exclaimed that one quarter of the meat would

---

[95]Ibid., p. 35.

be his alone—and Humayun agreed with a smiling 'very well'. In the meantime, other servants also jumped in to help. Later, the meat was divided as per the promise.[96]

Many years later, while appointing Jauhar as the Tehsildar of Haibatpur, Humayun told him the story of a dishonest Mughal who snatched a blanket from a poor man on the first day of his appointment as a collector. When the poor fellow protested against this exploitation, the new appointee replied—didn't the scoundrel know that the government had appointed him to 'collect'? Jauhar understood the sarcasm, and he records that on receiving this hint, he said, 'I am aware of my own unfitness for public employment, but trust that through your Majesty's favour and having had the honour for so many years of pouring water on the royal hands I shall not discredit the appointment to which I have been nominated.' The King replied, 'Good produces good, and evil causes evil.' He later reported to Humayun that in his pargana, people's wives and children were being enslaved by moneylenders because of the debts they were trapped in. He further informed that he had recovered hoarded grains concealed in deep dry wells, and they had been sold in the market. The money thus generated was used to repay the usurers and free people who were in their captivity. This pleased Humayun and he promoted Jauhar to a higher rank. The spontaneity of Jauhar's interactions with his master present a fine example of the latter's even-handedness.[97]

---

[96]Ibid., pp. 35–6.
[97]Ibid., pp. 112–13.

Once Humayun and his party were travelling through an area of such climatic contrasts that its summers roasted human bodies, and the winters froze them. It was terribly cold and so Humayun had one of his heavy fur coats unlined. He gave the top to Bairam Beg and the lining to Mehtar Anis. On another occasion, he unhesitatingly wore one of his assistant's clothes, which turned out to be from a lot that he had himself discarded earlier. Trousers presented to him by a poor old village woman were graciously accepted and worn. Indicators of Humayun's innate humility abound. He seems to have feared arrogance as a precursor of doom. When it was reported to him that Kamran was puffed with pride, all that he said was, 'Then his decline isn't far.' And indeed it wasn't.

A Thief and the Baadshah

Once, the royal party had to stay overnight in a hostile territory. They were totally worn out because all the wells which they had expected en route had been choked with sand by their opponents. Camps were pitched in a circular formation with camels on the outer periphery, followed by horses and then the tents in the centre. Humayun wanted to personally guard the site at night. However, a noble, Shaikh Ali, persuaded him to sleep for some time.

The next morning, Humayun was shocked to see that his sword, which he had used like a pillow, was half-drawn from its scabbard. He enquired of the servant sleeping in his tent whether he had touched it. The question jolted the shocked fellow not just out of his slumber but also his wits.

He retorted that he wouldn't dare indulge in such risky stupidity for anything in the world. The mystery was solved after many months, when a man boasting of his excellence in the art of thieving mentioned this episode in a market place and was overheard by Humayun's soldiers. He was immediately arrested and produced before the Baadshah, who not only pardoned him but also gave him some gifts. His largesse towards this thief implied two things—firstly, that he had considered what the fellow could have done to him as he slept, and secondly that his merciful approach could well have a reformative impact.[98]

Forgiveness: The Art of Setting Oneself Free

Humayun's command over the pen or the sword may not have been as meticulous as Babur's, but a skill at which he could match his father was the ability to let go.

Babur employed four of Ibrahim Lodi's cooks in his service, to have a taste of Hindustani cuisine. Someone tipped off the late Sultan's mother, and she conspired to have him poisoned. One of his tasters and a cook were bribed to carry out the plan. She personally sent some lethal chemicals for the job. On a Friday afternoon, when the toxic food was served, nothing amiss was noticed in the taste—but all those who consumed it began vomiting. In fact, Babur threw up on the dining cloth itself and ran vomiting all the way to the water cabinet. To confirm the murder attempt, a dog was fed some of the stuff and

---

[98]Ibid., p. 41.

it immediately took ill. When the ploy was tracked to Ibrahim's mother, Babur was quite surprised, since he had assigned a jagir and an honourable residence to her. The others involved in the conspiracy were liquidated, but the queen's life was spared. She was transferred to Kabul. By medieval standards, Babur had taken a lenient view.[99]

When Humayun reached Persia in January 1544 the monarch Shah Tahmasp had to take the call on handling his kingly guest, who at the moment wasn't exactly a king. The immediate hospitality that the Shah extended to Humayun was exceptionally grand, and his whole entourage was happy kicking their heels. However, the feasibility of a political and military alliance with him was still being debated amongst the royal bigwigs. Three noblemen—Raushan Beg Kukeh, who was Humayun's foster brother, Khawaja Ghazi Diwan and Sultan Mohammad—envenomed the Shah's mind against Humayun. The trio claimed that they could conquer Qandhar for the Shah with half of what the monarch would invest in refitting Humayun to do just that. Secondly, if the latter deserved any help, then his brothers would have surely helped him—and that there must have been a reason for their indifference towards him. Besides these suggestions, another matter which disoriented the Shah was the old, aforementioned intelligence report about the arrow-based divination. This had hurt his ego, and he now asked Humayun for a clarification. The Baadshah accepted his slip-up and said that since his empire was much larger than the domains of the Persian monarch, he

---

[99]*Gulbadan*, pp. 38–9.

had considered the Shah inferior to himself—however only God's will prevails. Rubbing in the irony that now he was forced to take refuge in the very place he had considered lowly, the Shah retorted with sarcasm that indeed, due to his foolish vanity, 'villagers' had driven him out of his 'vast empire'.[100]

However, the Shah's siblings managed to bring him around to support Humayun. His brother made a case on moral and ethical grounds and his sister, Shahzaadi Sultanam, on political ones. She pleaded that the Persian Empire had no dearth of antagonists—the Turks, the Uzbeks and others were perpetually on the lookout to devour it—thus they could very well do without adding the Mughals to this long list of foes. So there was no question of harming Humayun. However, if her brother did not intend to help him then he must clarify this immediately and ensure the guests' safe exit from Persia. The Shah was sagacious enough to value this counsel and he rightly understood that for the maintenance of a favourable balance of power in the region, it was critical to help Humayun.

The first step now was to snub the in-house opponents. The Shah felt that the three instigators mentioned earlier were diverting him from the path of dignity with their unworthy counsels and so they had to be put down—literally. Feet tied with rope and face first, they were to be lowered into a deep well called the Diwan of Suleiman. Their painfully slow death would have been an example to deter other challengers of this diplomatic coalition. As

---

[100] *Tazkirat-ul Waqiat*, pp. 69–70.

it happened, the ropes which were used to drop them at the bottom of the pit fell short, so they were hauled up only to be sent back down again the next morning. Making use of precious luck, Raushan Beg managed to send a petition to Humayun. Beg confessed his offence, implored forgiveness and begged the Baadshah to intercede for him to be pardoned by the Shah. In response, Humayun dispatched a supplication to Shah Tahmasp with a request to forgive the trio as an act of pious almsgiving, so that his late father, Shah Ismail's soul may rest in peace.[101] Despite his adamantine resolve in such matters, the Shah pardoned them. In admiration of Humayun's benign gesture he remarked that to forgive people who wish you death is not something that the weak can do. It needs exemplary forbearance and clemency—therefore his trust in this man's capabilities could not be misplaced. Indeed, he was right.

Circumstantial dynamics limit the options of forgiving and asking for forgiveness. Both need to be quick.

Valour and Values

When Humayun was marching back after his defeat at Chausa and was passing through Kalpi, the governor gave him some gifts. However, his intelligencers informed him that many more presents were supposed to be given to the Baadhshah, but due to his defeat, the Governor had lessened the offering. Hurt, Humayun returned all the gifts except one—an embroidered saddle which he thought

---

[101]Ibid., p. 72.

Kamran would like very much.[102] In 1541, when he was passing through Jodhpur and someone suggested that he should capture the place by launching a surprise attack on the local Raja, he replied, 'If you could make me king of the whole world I would not attempt so foul an action, or be guilty of such ingratitude.' On other occasions he had said: 'Good produces good and evil produces evil' and 'Pride must have a fall.'[103]

When Humayun was leaving for Persia, Akbar was left in the care of Askari. At that point, Aksari and Kamran were united against Humayun, but Akbar remained safe. Jauhar writes that when Humayun presented Akbar to Askari, the letter embraced the child lovingly, and further reports state that his wife treated the child with great affection. Kamran's act of using baby Akbar as a human shield when Humayun was besieging Kabul was considered sacrilege in the family circle. However, Humayun's reaction at the suggestion of eliminating Kamran is worth citing: 'No, never for the vanities of this perishable world will I imbrue my hands in the blood of a brother, but will forever remember the dying words of our respected parent who said to me "O Humayun! Beware, beware do not quarrel with your brothers, nor ever form any evil intentions towards them," these words are engraved on my heart forever.'[104]

Both Babur and Humayun are known to have visited the senior ladies of the harem on Fridays. Gulbadan reports

---

[102]Ibid., p. 19.
[103]Ibid., pp. 37, 113 & 89.
[104]Ibid., p 26.

that once Maham urged Babur to postpone his customary trip, since the weather was too hot. She suggested that this should not vex the ladies, since they too were aware of the climate. However, Babur not only overlooked the counsel but, in fact, he voiced shock at such a suggestion coming from Maham, who had known him for so long. He remarked that many of these ladies had lost their husbands and brothers, and if he didn't cheer them up, who would?[105] Likewise, Humayun was accosted by one of his wives, Bigeh Begum, in the presence of some senior ladies. Bolder than Maham, she questioned his partial allocation of time, which supposedly favoured the seniors. The complaint was peppered with a sarcastic enquiry thorns spread on the way to her residence? It was not unusual for pampered queens to bicker over the Baadshah's personal attention, but Humayun made a serious note of her comments. A meeting of the younger ladies of the harem was called. His wives and all others reported. His general silence had already announced that he was angry. With everyone in earshot he said, 'Bibi (Bigeh Begum), what ill treatment at my hands did you complain of this morning?... That was not the place to make a complaint. You know that I have been to the quarters of the elder relations of you all... It is a necessity laid on me to make them happy. Nevertheless I am ashamed before them because I see them so rarely...'[106] He made it quite clear to all the ladies that complaints

---

[105]*Exploring Medieval India Sixteenth to Eighteenth Centuries*, Vol-II, Meena Bhargava (edited), Orient Black Swan, New Delhi, 2010, p. 242.
[106]Ibid.

of this nature were not appreciated, and advised them to be content and grateful with whatever time he could spend with them. It is likely that the younger ladies of the harem would have had many diversions to keep them engaged, but for the older lot, the Baadshah's visit might have been a relatively rare occasion of celebration. Besides, his attention would have been a priceless reassurance. If the overenthusiasm for attaching political meaning to every word is curbed, this practice comes across simply as a value system of giving the old their due. The rights of the senior members of the family were upheld as sacrosanct.

If someone ever said that good books make great tutors, he was completely correct. Humayun was not a great writer, but he was an avid reader. In fact, even when he was fleeing for his life from Sher Shah, he ensured that his books were loaded on a camel. During the journey, like most of his possessions, the books were also lost, but luckily the camel carrying them just happened to find its way back and the Baadshah read this as a sign of good fortune.

Thus Humayun's attitude towards life could be summed up in a positive 'So what!' He trusted easily, was deceived easily, forgave easily, thanked easily and allowed himself to hope despite anguish, love despite hostilities, and above all, welcome happiness with open arms—however, whenever and wherever it dropped by.

Chapter V

Shielding the Show: Sher Shah—A Manager Par Excellence

When you were ten years old and someone asked you what you wanted to be when you grew up, anything seemed possible. Astronaut. Archaeologist. Fireman. Baseball player. The first female President of the United States. Your answers then were guided by what you thought would make you really happy. There were no limits. There are a determined few who never lose sight of aspiring to do something that's truly meaningful to them. But for many of us, as the years go by, we allow our dreams to be peeled away. We pick our jobs for the wrong reasons and then we settle for them. We begin to accept that it's not realistic to do something we truly love for a living. Too many of us who start down the path of compromise will never make it back... A strategy—whether in companies or in life-is created through hundreds of everyday decisions about how you spend your time, energy, and money. With every moment of your time, every decision about how you spend your energy and your money, you are making a statement about what really matters to you. You can talk all you want about having a clear purpose and strategy for your life, but ultimately it means nothing if you are not investing the resources you have in a way that is consistent with your strategy. In the end, a strategy is nothing but good intentions unless effectively implemented.

-CLAYTON M. CHRISTENSEN, *How Will You Measure Your Life*[107]

Timeline: Fiteenth-sixteenth century CE

Backdrop: Farid Khan, aka Sher Shah Suri, was an Afghan monarch who ruled over parts of northern India from 1540 to 1545. Abbas Khan Sarwani, a contemporary, writes that Farid's father, Miyan Hasan, had eight sons. Farid and his full brother Nizam were born of an Afghan wife, Ali and Yusuf of another wife, Khurram and Shadi Khan of another, and Sulayman and Ahmad of the fourth wife. Miyan Hasan had no love, affection and regard for Farid's mother, but was very well disposed towards his slave girls and was especially attached to his fourth wife. He was so captivated by her charms that she practically ruled over him.[108] Thus, being the son of a discriminatory and neglectful father, Sher Shah grew up to be a man of high-impact resilience.

---

[107]Clayton M. Christensen, James Allworth, Karen Dillon, *How Will You Measure Your Life*, Harper Collins Publishers, London, 2012, pp. 21 and 74–75.
[108]Abbas Khan Sarwani, *Tarikh-i Sher Shahi*, Vol-II, S.M. Imam al-Din (edited and translated), University of Dacca, Dacca, 1964, pp. 8–9.

Farid Khan built the Afghan Empire from humble beginnings and climbed the ladder of ascendency one rung at a time, without losing balance. His focus on his dreams remained as steady as steady can be. His grandfather Ibrahim was probably a horse trader who migrated from Roh to Hindustan during the reign of Bahlol Lodi (1451–1489). He was employed by Jamal Khan, an Afghan officer, at Hissar Firoza. Later, his son Hasan, Farid Khan's father, was confirmed at the same designation. Farid's first step was acquiring academic proficiency at Jaunpur (1494–1497).[109] He studied Arabic and Persian and had a special liking for History and the study of biographies. This was followed by the efficient management of his father's jagir at Sasaram (1497–1518). Abbas Khan Sarwani reports that Hasan was apprised of the strategy that Farid would employ to administer his jagirs, in the following words:

> Administering justice is the best means of ensuring the prosperity of a country, the expansion of a kingdom, the filling up of treasury and the increase of the population of villages and towns. Injustice is most pernicious. It saps the foundation of government, it brings ruin to the realm and earns bad name in this world and the world to come. Prosperity of a kingdom depends on two things: First, affection to subjects in general and kindness towards all people. The weak are the trust of God given to the charge of the powerful so that under their protection they may remain safe from the assault of the tyrants and the

---

[109]Ibid., pp. 9–10.

torture of the oppressors. Secondly, administration of justice is incumbent because the prosperity of the country depends on good administration ...When the tyrants and the seditious persons see the fire of punishment flaming they retire into seclusion. If there is slackness in the matter of administration numerous rebellions break out, sedition sets in everywhere and the foundation of the state is jolted. It has been said by the wise persons that a state is a plant and the administration, water and hence it is incumbent upon the ruler to keep the root of the tree of government alive by watering it so that the fruit of peace and tranquility may appear.[110]

Next, he worked in the employ of the various bigwigs of his times like Daulat Khan Lodi (1519), Bahadur Khan Nuhani (1526) and Junaid Barlas (1527). He served in the Mughal army as well, and happened to accompany Babur on his Chanderi expedition (1528). Babur assigned him a jagir in 1528–29. Later, he became the deputy of Jalal Khan, the minor ruler of Bihar, and dominated the political scenario at his court (1529). The exposure to Mughal military organization stood him in good stead. Gradually, he rose to prominence as an upcoming Afghan leader. His ambitions grew because of his sway over Bihar and Bengal, and eventually he became a threat to the Mughal ruler Humayun, who could hardy match his skills at being foxy and lupine in shifting political strategies. Ultimately, after years of hide and seek and much harassment, the Mughal

---

[110]Ibid., pp. 11–12.

Baadshah was defeated by him in two consecutive battles at Chausa (1539) and Kannauj (1540). Humayun not only lost his empire, he was barely able to escape with his life.

Although Sher Shah's reign lasted only a few years, his impact on the administrative system of north India was lasting. He dewaxed the sluggish and corrupt officials who robbed the government with one hand and the peasantry with the other. The modalities of revenue assessment and collection were reformed. He recommended that raids by the auditors of the revenue collectors' accounts should be surprise checks. The relevant papers of the village should be seized by the auditors before the village headman was warned of such a raid.[111] His insistence on 'daagh-o-chehra' (branding of horses maintained by individuals and nobles and maintenance of descriptive rolls of soldiers) improved the efficiency of the army. Officials were called to account for crimes in their areas and were personally obliged to compensate the victims. Abbas Khan Sarwani informs that the duties of the village 'muqaddam' (headman) went far beyond the management of village finances. He was held accountable for any crime that happened within his village or near it. In cases of robbery or murder of travellers, he was obliged to produce the culprits and the goods stolen.[112] Irfan Habib calls it a 'rough and ready' system of maintaining law and order, which was continued by the Mughals.[113]

---

[111] Irfan Habib, *The Agrarian System of Mughal India 1556–1707*, Second Revised Edition, Oxford University Press, 1999, p. 323
[112] Ibid. p. 163
[113] Ibid., p. 164.

Sher Shah also commissioned the construction of a network of roads to facilitate trade and commerce. Trees were planted to keep them cool and Dak Khanas (post offices), 'serais' (motels) and 'thanas' (police check-posts) were made at regular intervals. Free trade was opened between the various provinces of the empire. He refined the coinage system and insisted on the purity of the coins produced from his mints. His silver 'rupiya' continued as a standard coin for centuries after him.

Intermediaries who towed the line of Sher Shah's efficient and honest administration were retained, while those who were found to be habitually contumacious and repeat offenders were given exemplary punishments. Habib informs us that when Sher Shah was managing his father's jagir in Bihar, the rebellious zamindars of that area were ruthlessly eliminated. In fact, the foot-troopers of such zamindars, called the 'ganwaars' (local peasants), were also uprooted and completely new people were settled in such villages to smoothen the flow of obedience.[114] Leniency was shown at the time of assessment of tax, but no concessions were allowed at the time of collection. Every city and fort was equipped with military supplies and treasures. Land revenue assignments were granted to officers for a steady maintenance of troops which could be summoned to service with the royal forces.

However, money accorded to the nobility was no guarantee of a competent army. Corrupt officials pocketed the funds allocated for the salary of regular soldiery and

---

[114]Ibid., p. 206

hired untrained people as and when necessity arose. Ensuring that as many soldiers were on an officer's payroll as he claimed put the states' efficiency to test. The rigorous implementation of daagh-o-chehra was the only way to check fraud and have a committed army. Thus paraphernalia of officials like 'karkuns' (clerks), 'chihradars' (maintainers of the descriptive rolls), 'aspkhaanadars' (in-charge of stables), 'pheeldaars' (in-charge of elephants), 'khazanadaars' (treasurers), 'toofangdaars' (matchlock men), 'kotwals' (officer-in-charge of law and order), 'shiqdaars' (officer in charge of a unit of administration) and 'munsifs' (judge of a unit of administration) etc. were employed to work collectively towards good governance. Officers like the Shiqdaar-i shiqdaaraan and Munsif-i munsifaan were appointed for a higher level of review of applications and of the work of officers of subordinate units. Thus a bureaucracy with a reasonably neat system of hierarchy was put in place.

His reforms testified to his dexterity in administration and politics and many of his data and systems were retained and further refined by Akbar. The *Ain-i-Akbari* records the initiation of the gaz-i Ilaahi unit of land measurement in 1586 and the unit used before that is recorded as the gaz-i Sikandari/Iskandari. The latter name is associated with Sikandar Lodi (1489–1519), who had initiated the use of this unit of measurement. However, some documents from Sher Shah's period mention another unit called the gaz-i Sher Shahi, which implies that Sher Shah had made enough changes in the gaz-i Sikandari/Iskandari for the unit to be given his name.[115] The crop rates fixed by Sher Shah have also been mentioned by Abul Fazl. He states that the Sur ruler had brought Hindustan under the Zabt system of revenue management. Rai (crop rates) were fixed for lands which were 'Polaj' (under continuous cultivation) or 'Parauti' (left fallow very rarely). Rai was based on three rates, depending on the quantum of yield: good, average or low. An average of these was taken to arrive at a general rate of the produce, and a third of that amount was fixed as the tax. In the initial year of Akbar's reign, Sher Shah's Rai rates were used to assess taxes.[116]

Given the shortness of his reign, his contribution to architecture also remarkable. He built the Purana Qila, which was intended to be the sixth city of Delhi. The architecture of the Qila-i Kuhna mosque (1542), which is located within the Purana Qila, is unique. However, it is his tomb at Sasaram which is considered to be an architectural masterpiece. It is set in a tank and can be approached by a causeway. The tomb has five vertical stages and the design changes sharply at each stage. The conception is absolutely free of the influence of any other building.

The anecdotes presented here highlight the ruler's pragmatic approach to administration and his zest for excellence.

◆

---

[115]Ibid. p. 406.
[116]Ibid. pp. 240–1.

Looking Beyond Looks: A Word for Recruiters

Whenever possible, Sher Shah supervised the daagh-o-chehra personally and settled wages of old and new recruits. On one such occasion a youth approached him, riding a high breed-horse and dressed chicly, he was a picture of flamboyance. However, Sher Shah fixed a rather low remuneration for him. Shaikh Khalil, a Sufi, interceded on the youth's behalf and said that he deserved a better salary. To defend his decree the king asked the young man to draw his bow. The fellow couldn't draw it that enough to shoot an arrow. It implied that either he was too weak or out of practice, or he simply didn't know how to do it. Nevertheless, the Sufi argued that the bow was possibly new and stiff, and that is why it could not be drawn properly. In response, Sher Shah ordered his personal bow to be brought. This one was soft due to regular use in practicing. But the man failed to draw this one as well. Now the Sufi interceded that his stifling and heavy suit of armour was an impediment to the test. So the king generously allowed another trial without the suit, but he failed yet again.

Sher Shah concluded that military trials should be conducted with a view to establishing a candidate's ability and sincerity. Not only did recruiting incompetent men compromise the cumulative strength of the army, the life of such men would be at greater risk than usual in the battlefield. Well-dressed people, who were suave and deferential, could also turn out to be surprising failures. He warned recruiters that outwardly charming and inwardly shallow men might be able to attract promiscuous women, but before granting a commission they should assess if the candidates were up to scratch, all cosmetic excesses notwithstanding.[117]

Thus the king emphasized the idea that the suitability of a candidate is a very critical factor. For example, beautiful-looking lips are not essential for delivering a great talk—however, they might be totally indispensible if one has to sell lipstick.

Official Records and Tools of Governance

Once, a soldier appeared before Sher Shah and tried to pass muster by cheating. He was one amongst several temporary fillers hired by a noble to act as ghost soldiers. The king picked up the soldier's sly vibes and inquired as to where and by whom had he been recruited. The soldier lied that the king had mustered him himself at Manikpur. The poor fellow was probably unaware that officers maintained detailed muster books, and therefore particulars of the Manikpur muster were, in fact, available. So he was asked to furnish details about the date and name of the village where he was interviewed. Obviously he failed, and begged the king's forgiveness. He was promised amnesty if he disclosed the name of the official who had tutored him to lie. Eventually, all the fraudulent enrollers were apprehended. This particular man was forgiven and

---

[117]Shaikh Rizqullah Mushtaqui, *Waqiat-i Mushtaqi*, Iqtidar Husain Siddiqui (translated and edited), Indian Council of Historical Research and Northern Book Centre, New Delhi, 1992, pp. 139–40.

properly recruited as a soldier.[118]

The deceit was plotted on the assumption that two years had passed since the monarch's Manikpur inspection, and therefore details for cross-referencing would not be available. However, records were maintained and they had duplicates in Persian and Hindawi. The man who gave two rupees to someone to act as a soldier and charged the government hundreds on the pretext of the soldier's salary could not get away with the trick, because someone else had done his homework, and done it well.

As noted before, Sher Shah recommended that the person sent to audit the accounts of the village officials (amils) should conduct a surprise raid so that the papers could not be changed or manipulated by the local revenue officials and the village headmen. Medieval records refer to cases where the Kaaghaz-i asli/Kaaghaz-i khaam (original/old records of villages' revenue) were burnt and replaced with new manipulated papers to deceive auditors.

Recruitment of a 'Nobody'

Once, when Sher Shah was deciding the selection of candidates for armed services, a rather naive young man appeared for the interview. The monarch dismissed him, calling him a 'nobody' under his breath. The poor fellow overheard him and asked the superintendent what pay a 'nobody' could expect. The superintendent smiled at his and the king, having noticed that, asked him the reason for

---

[118]Ibid., p. 141.

his smile. When he was informed about the interviewee's enquiry, he couldn't help laughing. Moved by the man's gullibility and innocence, he actually gave him employment. So he loosened the straps of power whenever he could, and walked down the slant of the human side.[119]

The Charwadaar and the Observant Monarch

During one of his inspectorial visits, Sher Shah noticed that a rider looked conspicuously uncomfortable. He asked the man to dismount from his horse. Troubled by the order, the man fell off, awkward and inelegant. The monarch enquired whether he was a soldier or the just the groomer of the horse, because his posture indicated that he was not proficient at riding. Scared out of his wits, he confessed that, in fact, he was only the 'charwadaar' (the one who feeds the horse) and had been paid by an official to pose as a regular cavalry man. The perpetrator of the bogus presentation was punished, but the poor man was forgiven.

Thus Sher Shah discouraged slipshod surveying methods and was serious about weeding out the parasitic existence of unfair functionaries. Enthusiasm was a key element in his style of management and a very potent catalyst, which mixed with his ability, produced energy—positive energy.[120]

---

[119]Ibid., pp. 141–42.
[120]Ibid., p. 141.

Resolution of Unanticipated Problems

One afternoon, when Sher Shah was engrossed in administrative affairs, he heard a voice other than that of the Muizzen's (one who calls for prayers in a mosque) calling out the Zuhar azaan (call for the afternoon prayer). The interloper added a line which was standard in the Fajr azaan (call for the dawn prayers)—'There is greater benefit in prayer than in sleep.' This atypical call attracted the king's attention and the man was summoned in his presence. He inquired whether the bizarre reference to the benefits of being awake in the afternoon implied that the man had assumed that the king slept throughout the day. The audaciously affirmative answer came rather pat. He said that had the king been awake, he would be knowledgeable about the caller's misery. When the king retorted that this accusation was unfair since his officers were charged with easing people's burdens, the man claimed that his officials were unapproachable—at least for him. The king replied that in this case, he should have brought the matter to the royal notice directly, since an open court for subjects was held regularly. The man complained that the guards would not have allowed him to come close enough to the king to make a direct representation, and that he had to beg for food to survive till this day. The king now asked why he had not taken food from the free kitchen run under the aegis of the royal treasury, because it was being funded to discourage people from begging. The man said that he did not want to leave the palace gates even for a moment, therefore begging from the adjoining houses was more convenient. It was evident that the fellow was a chronic complainer. He had practised complaining so much that where a layman would see no fault, he, the expert, could see many. Disgusted by his habit of finding problems in every solution, the king ordered that he should be whipped and put in the prison. This was to teach him patience. However, after sometime, when the king's crossness wore off, he called the man to the presence chamber and ordered that he be given rupees corresponding to the number of whiplashes he had received. Then he was asked to state his petition. The man appealed for the restoration of the lands which he had previously held as a revenue-free assignment, as his allotment had been recently revoked. While representing his case before the king, the man now restrained his ill humour. The lashing and a couple of hours in jail had taught him that things could always get worse, and therefore it is important to adopt a positive and grateful outlook towards all situations. The king conveyed that life is full of surprises, but one should not be so surprised as to see catastrophe in every change. Convinced that the man's grouchiness had been shaken off, the king granted his wish, and to compensate for his own snappish reaction, ordered that his travel expenses back to his home town Radauli (Barabanki, Uttar Pradesh) be covered by the state.[121] Thus Sher Shah tried to strike a balance between rigidity and plasticity, and although he had a top-down approach, he never ignored what lay at the ground level.

On the basis of evidence coming from Abbas Khan

---

[121]Ibid., pp. 142–43.

Sarwani, Irfan Habib records that the use of corruption and fraud in obtaining Madad-i maash land grants was so common, that Sher Shah was compelled to take measures to protect the state from forged alterations in the farmans.[122] The nature of these grants was such that the grantee did not have full proprietary rights over the land. The assignment was held by him only for such time as the emperor pleased. Although, usually, the grant was left undisturbed with in the lifetime of the grantee, the right to resume the grant was always reserved with the king. A lot of land grants were cancelled on the suspicion that they had been obtained by corrupt and fraudulent means. It is important to note that Sher Shah wanted the Madad-i maash land holders to contribute in some way beyond their socio-religious role. Habib writes that one of Sher Shah's farmans commanded that the holders should offer all the five prayers in congregation in the mosque, and discharge ten arrows each after the Zuhr prayers.[123] This order seems to have had more than religious connotation. Firstly, regular public appearances meant that if a holder was absent for some reason, the absence would have been noted by a lot of people immediately, and accordingly the allotment of the grant would have been reviewed by the concerned officials. Secondly, regular gatherings would have created awareness about the people and issues around them, and that would have been of help in case of an inquisition. Finally, the practice of archery would have

---

[122]*The Agrarian System of Mughal India*, p. 349
[123]Ibid. p. 358.

made them capable of helping the state officials against local criminals. So he wanted to rub in the fact that there are no free lunches, and that one has to be grateful for whatever one has—free or paid.

Situating Justice in Religion

Abbas Khan Sarwani informs about Sher Shah's views on justice in the following words:

> If the ruler finds out that any one of them (officers/ administrators) has indulged in tyranny and oppression and rebellion, be it his son even, he should disgrace and penalize him and restrain him from it strictly and harshly. He should not be lenient and kind in this respect; rather he should compel him to compensate the loss suffered by the victim. In this he should not make any concessions for his relations, attendants and courtiers because a tyrant is actually an enemy of the ruler on two grounds: Firstly because the fear of the ruler and the respect of his State disappear and he is considered low, indolent and unjust among his subjects. Secondly, because the subjects withdraw their hands from cultivation they become rather indifferent... Justice is the most excellent of religious rites, impeccable justice is incumbent in all religions and is approved alike by the kings of the infidels as well as the believers. There is no devotion in prayer equal to justice, which is deserved equally by all the communities of the unbelievers and the faithful. If the

shadow of royal justice is removed from the head of the people, the tie of unity and prosperity is loosened and the strong and powerful men annihilate the weak. And whatever occurs to mind is reflected in the actions of the courtiers and becomes the cause of the decline of the Kingdom. On account of worldly greediness there should not be excess of avarice for the share of soldiers and subjects on the strength of power, portion and abundance, of soldiers and attendants and should avoid the arrow of deep sigh of the oppressed.

If your arrow passes through the steel armlet (coat of mails)

(Beware) *The javelin of sigh* (of the oppressed) *passes through the mountain of iron.*[124]

---

[124] *Tarikh-i Sher Shahi*, pp. 12 and 159.

Chapter VI

The Last Word: An Equilibrial Mantra, Sulh-i kul

Marx has said that religious world is the reflex of the real world, and Max Weber tended, at least in part, to invert this notion to emphasize the development of ideology, ideas and ethics as factors behind economic and social development. For example, the rational spirit was seen by him as crucial for the development of capitalism. One need not, however, accept Weber's 'inversion' in order to stress the importance of ideology in history, which Marx too did not deny. At this level too Akbar made a contribution by invoking reason and questioning established beliefs... Dedication to Sulh-i kul implied that steps should be carried out to impress upon everyone the main spiritual truth that religious quarrels are not to be permitted. This task it was now argued, could be successful only under a sovereign who is the vicegerent of God. Akbar and Abu'l Fazl built up a theory of sovereignty which had two pillars. One of the concept of 'Social Contract', which Abu'l Fazl put forward in his chapter, rawa-i rozi, that was very similar to the 'Theory of Social Contract' becoming *popular in Europe in the 17th century... The other pillar of sovereignty was that just as God does not withhold the rays of the sun and the rain from those who do not believe in him, so the King too, as God's representative, cannot hold back his bounties on the basis of differences of faith.*

IRFAN HABIB, *Akbar And His Age*[125]

Timeline: 1556–1605

Backdrop: Sulh-i kul (Absolute Peace/Universal Peace) was the sum total of Jalaluddin Muhammad Akbar's reign and life. It was during his time that the Mughals were internalized in the spirit of India, like whiteness in milk or the inimitable fragrance that accompanies wet mud.

Babur and Humayun, Akbar's grandfather and father respectively, were men of remarkable qualities, though of different types. Babur was intelligent, shrewd, hard-working and determined. Relatively, Humayun was naive and easy-going, but the fact that he regained his lost empire and the Sur interregnum was undone is in itself a proof of his abilities. Both of them were emotional in personal relationships and generous in professional ones. Their insistence on equity and kindness against the general backdrop of their times was exceptional. However neither of them ruled long enough to leave a traceable mark on the lifestyle of their domains. Akbar was the man destined to

---

[125]Cf. *Akbar And His Age*, Iqtidar Alam Khan (edited), Northern Book Centre, New Delhi, 1999, pp. xii–xiii.

do that. Much ahead of his times, he broke rules to make new ones—and indeed, some of them were better than those that he broke.

◆

Pieces of the Jigsaw

1542: Akbar is born.

1545: He is reunited with his parents.

1556: Ascends the throne.

1556–1560: He is dominated by his ataliq (advisor) Bairam Khan.

1561–1575: Ontogenesis of political alliances with Indian Muslims and Rajputs.

1562: Akbar visits the shrine of Khwaja Muinuddin Chishti at Ajmer and initiates sociopolitical agreements with the Rajputs, alongside an understanding with Amber.

1562–67: Five years and five great rebellions:

Revolt of Mirza Sharfuddin—1562

Revolt of Shah Abul Maali—1564

Revolt of Abdullah Khan—1564

Revolt of Ali Quli Khan—1565–67

Asaf Khan's desertion—1565-66

Revolt of the Mirzas—1566

1562-67: Improvement in the position of Persian Shia nobility.

1562: Abolition of the custom of enslaving prisoners of war.

1563: Abolition of Pilgrimage Tax and execution of Adham Khan.

1564-65: Sheikh Abdun Nabi appointed as the Sadr (central minister in charge of revenue-free grants).

1564: Abolition of Jazia.

1565: Akbar lays the foundation of a new fort at Agra.

1565: Inam grants for temples begin and continue. Todar Mal and Muzaffar Khan Turbati begin to manage the Empire's Ministry of Finance.

1568: Fatehnama of Chittor.

1568-1579: Akbar visits Ajmer regularly during this phase.

1569: Birth of Prince Salim.

1571: Commencement of building work at Sikri.

1573: Project of translating Sanskrit works into Persian begins. Conquest of Gujarat and Sikri renamed Fatehabad.

1574-75: Major revenue reforms—State's revenue demand is recalculated and fixed in cash.

1575: Reimposition of Jazia.

1575–81: Ibadat Khana (House of prayers) debates and discussions.

1579: Issue of Mahzar and banishment of Abdun Nabi and Makhdum ul Mulk.

1580: New system of territorial division of the empire is initiated. Mansabdari system is further refined. Jazia re-abolished. Nauroz festivities are revived. Akbar breaks off with the orthodoxy and withdraws patronage to sections which oppose the idea of Sulh-i kul.

1580–1605: Sulh-i kul reigns.

1582: Akbar liberates his personal slaves, who are now called chela.

1583: He condemns Sati and rescues a widow himself.

1585: Capital is shifted to Lahore and the Emperor leaves Fatehpur Sikri.

1586: Abul Fazl is commissioned to write a detailed official history, thus we get the *Akbarnama/A'in-i Akbari*.

1589: *Akbarnama* is completed but improvements and additions continue till the author's assassination in 1601.

1601: Akbar returns to Agra.

1605: Akbar dies at Agra.

♦

Bairam Khan's Containment: A Genii Bottled

Humayun's accidental death in January 1556 seemed particularly ill-timed. The recovery of the empire was recent and the power broth was terribly undercooked. Mubariz Khan Sur (Adil Shah) and Hemu, his accomplished commander, were mobilizing the Afghans of Eastern India to collaborate with them for a grand anti-Mughal offensive. The Mughals were already worried about Hemu's professional skills and the numerical strength of his forces, but Humayun's death aggravated their perturbation. The Afghans were enthused to expedite action and press for early combat. Fourteen-year-old Akbar was at Kalanaur (Gurdaspur) when Humayun died, and his senior loyalists were shrewd enough to arrange for the prince's immediate coronation. In the face of the Afghan threat, Bairam Khan, Akbar's ataliq (advisor), was unanimously accepted as the Wakil-us Sultanate by all the nobles. But some of them were uncomfortable at the sudden empowerment of one of their colleagues. Later developments proved their fears correct. Nevertheless, veterans like Tardi Beg, Munim Beg, Khizr Khwaja Khan, Khwaja Jalaluddin Mahmud and Khwaja Muazzam etc. realized that confrontations in the inner circle at this critical time might cost them the empire itself. Therefore, they ignored Bairam Khan's airs and their own claims to the Wikalat, and thought it prudent to stand united under his leadership—at least till such time as the danger from Hemu had passed. The tales of Humayun's hazardous flight from Hindustan were perhaps too nagging to be forgotten and nobody wanted a repetition of that history. Of course, they couldn't have done anything wiser, because Hemu indeed was a formidable contender.

Bairam Khan used this situation to build a personal power base. He pursued a deliberate policy of exclusion of the bigwigs who had been at the core of Humayun's nobility. Some of them, like Shah Abul Ma 'ali, Bapus Beg and Tulak Khan Quchin, were removed from the political stage. Others like Shamsuddin Muhammad Atka and Muhammad Quli Khan Barlas etc. were sent away to Kabul. He also tried to keep Munim Khan, the governor of Kabul, entangled in local issues so that he would not exercise any influence on the politics of the central court and Akbar could be kept isolated from various influences.[126]

The dreaded Afghan offensive came in October 1556. In the first round of combat, the Mughals were defeated in the battle of Tughluqabad. Tardi Beg, who was in command, was keen on a quick engagement with the Afghans because he wanted to prove his worth in the battlefield before the Wakil's arrival. The wary Bairam Khan was uneasy with precisely this possibility. Accordingly, a faithful supporter, Pir Muhammad Khan, was sent on the field to ensure that the battle was not fought and won in his absence. The backup forces were also delayed. So, despite the compromises that the Mughal nobility had made to defeat Hemu, they were defeated. This outcome disturbed the balance of power not just in the Mughal–Afghan context but also in the Mughal–Mughal context. Of course the

---

[126]Iqtidar Alam Khan, *India's Polity in the Age of Akbar*, Permanent Black and Ashoka University, Ranikhet, 2016, pp. 93–100.

tilt was in the Wakil's favour because it highlighted that his personal excellence was critical to the survival of the empire.

Tardi Beg had stood by Humayun throughout his trials, though unwillingly at times. Abul Fazl reports that on the day of the lost battle, divisiveness overflowed from the Mughal camp. The cowards were hesitant to fight out of fear, the brave hesitated out of caution, and Tardi's enthusiasm for a quick and decisive clash lay in distant political concerns resting outside the battlefield—perhaps in the central court. Defiance and smugness were nothing new for him. It was well known that he was a haughty hot spur who had tested Humayun's humility time and again. While the Baadshah always forgave him, his colleague did not. Despite the fact that Tardi had trusted the Wakil enough to hand over the custody of Mirza Kamran's son Mirza Abul Qasim to him, the latter had him executed on unjust and superfluous charges of treason. Leaving the field to save one's life in the face of imminent defeat/death and then reporting to the central command for further directions wasn't quite treason by medieval standards, but that is exactly how it was interpreted by Bairam Khan. On the witness of Pir Muhammad Khan and Ali Quli Khan, Tardi was executed on 22 October 1556, without a formal sanction from Akbar.[127]

The nobility received a severe jolt. Bairam Khan used money and power to suppress any serious and open condemnation of the act. For example, Maham Anga,

---

[127]Ibid., p. 101.

Akbar's chief wet nurse and an influential person in the harem, was bribed. Tardi's loyalists like Khwaja Sultan Ali, Mir Asghar Munshi and Khanjer Beg were imprisoned. Special care was taken to prevent the leakage of this news at Kabul, where senior nobles and close associates of the assassinated noble were stationed. It was made officially public only after a month of the second battle of Panipat (5 November 1556) and the Mughal victory therein.[128]

It became apparent that Bairam Khan was eliminating veterans so that he could reconstitute the Mughal team under his personal leadership. His friends, like Ali Quli Khan Uzbek, Husain Quli Khan and Abdullah Khan Uzbek etc, were promoted to important positions. When the news of Tardi's assassination was broken to Munim Khan after three months, it sounded more like an injunction than information. Within six months of the execution, Bairam had practically isolated the young Baadshah and was looking forward to being the de facto ruler.

Akbar's mother Hamida Banu was young, but she had been Humayun's partner in his political trials and that experience stood her in good stead. Supported by loyalists like Munim Khan, she was determined to halt Bairam's blitzkrieg. Generally speaking, the royal ladies received power and wealth through a channel of male relations: father/husband/son etc. Therefore, Hamida's worries over Akbar's subservience to Bairam Khan were understandable for more reasons than one. She fixed his marriage with the granddaughter of Munim Khan, a rival of the Wakil, and

---

[128]Ibid., 102–3.

a grand wedding ceremony was organized to drive home to the latter that the royalty did not need his approval to do what they wanted to do. Although Maham Anga had initially supported Bairam Khan, she distanced herself from him after Hamida's arrival from Kabul (April–August 1557).[129]

Though Bairam Khan had earned Humayun's gratitude for his unflinching support in tough times, it was definitely not in his capacity to dominate the late Baadshah's family. An attempt was made on the Wakil's life at Mankot when untamed elephants rushed towards him (1557).[130] He was alarmed and angry, but his addiction to power continued. He tried to stabilize his position by the inclusion of some important nobles in the dominating clique. It was agreed that he would not have the exclusive right of placing proposals before Akbar. The nobles would meet twice a week and decisions would be taken in consensus (April 1558). But most members of the Wakil's club were sycophants and opportunists, so the moment he slipped clumsily on the path of ascendency, they applied the reverse gear and drove straight into Akbar's camp.

Akbar, in any case, was a genius politician and could not have been overshadowed for too long. Eventually, with the support of the harem and the nobility, he bottled the genii into the lamp (1560). Thus denuded of power and dumped by supporters, Bairam Khan set off for Mecca—supposedly on his own will—but was assassinated in

---

[129]Ibid., pp. 107–8.
[130]Ibid., p. 109.

Gujarat, on the way (1561). It is interesting to note that his son Muhammad Rahim Mirza was brought up under Akbar's personal attention and affection. His widow Salima Sultan Begum was married to Akbar. She was also a cousin of his by virtue of being a granddaughter of Babur through one of his daughters.

Shireen Moosvi cites Muhammad Arif Qandhari's *Tarikh-i Akbari* to present a letter that Akbar wrote to Bairam Khan after his dismissal. The latter's relationship with the Baadshah is compared with the unbreakable bond between a father and son. The tone of the letter is remarkably polite:

> My Khan Baba! Let him read our letter of affectionate greetings and message of love, and know that, previous to this, owing to certain facts and circumstances we have encamped at Delhi. When we heard that you were coming to wait on us, we sent Tarsun Beg (to say) that, since we had received much grief and hurt from you, it is not proper that you should at this time wait on us, but should remain as you are and deal with affairs as require attention. If the need arises, we will come to Agra. You may go in advance to Gwalior and that territory, so that whenever we summon you, you can wait upon us. For reassuring you, we had written that though there may arise a quarrel between father and son, yet neither can be indifferent to each other. Since you are our Khan Baba, the same relationship applies between us. In spite of this grief and hurt and improper and unworthy act (from you), we hold you

in our affection, and favour and love you. We still call you and recognize you as 'Khan Baba' as in the past.[131]

Iqtidar Alam Khan rightly notes that the crisis leading to Bairam Khan's exit was perhaps the first round of the struggle between the central authority and forces operating in the opposite direction within the Mughal polity.[132] The Wakil's assertion had left such a deep gash on the central flesh of governance that it was quickly infected with sedition. Thus some nobles assumed that they deserved an unaccountable share in the freshly re-recovered Mughal dominion. Though Bairam Khan was subjugated, the legacy of assertion which he handed down to the nobility was difficult to reverse. No wonder Akbar had to grapple with many serious revolts (1562–1567). Thus, where assertive officers saw their right, he saw an infringement of his authority. The nobility's dalliance with defiance was damned, and he crushed centrifugal inclinations with exceptional courage.

Akbar could not have banked on the Sunni Muslim nobility, because they proved to be the most ungovernable. The Afghans had been displaced by the Mughals, so they were resentful and unreliable. Therefore he gave positions of trust to Indian non-Muslims and Muslims, and a large number of Shia Muslims of non-Indian origin. This reinvention filled the political vacuum and neutralized the power of contumacious elements. He experimented with

---

[131]Shireen Moosvi, *Episodes in the Life of Akbar Contemporary Records and Reminiscences*, National Book Trust, New Delhi, 1994, p. 19.
[132]*India's Polity in the Age of Akbar*, pp. 116–17.

ideas and people and thereafter selected the best options available to even out disagreements. Of course, conditions kept changing, and so the experiments continued. They stopped only when everything reached a state of equilibrium—the political, the social, and the personal. Acceptance budded from the seeds of toleration and finally bloomed as a celebration of differences. Akbar freed the idea of alliance from all boundaries and agendas, and embedded it human minds as a partnership in humanness. He worked towards minimization of conflicts in every area of human existence. This was his final policy, both political and personal, and he remained committed to it till the end. This mantra of equilibrium was Sulh-i kul.

◆

Tracking Tolerance

Akbar probed into open-mindedness from the very beginning of his career. However, his secular views surfaced clearly sometime around 1580. Thereafter, his acceptance of and respect for other faiths was so unconditional that the voice of orthodoxy, Abdul Qadir Badaoni, and the Christian Jesuits declared that perhaps he was not a Muslim. Shaikh Ahmad Sarhindi went a step further and claimed that Akbar had not only deviated from Islam, but he hated it.

A simple explanation for Akbar's liberalitsm is often located in the claim that his mother was a Shia and therefore he was exposed to the idea of balancing differences of creed from early childhood. However,

Iqtidar Alam Khan opines that Hamida was not a Shia, since her brother Mu'azzam Beg was involved in the assassination of Humayun's Shia Wazir Khwaja Sultan Rushdi (1546), and the killing was understood to be the design of orthodox Sunni bigots. This shifts the focus towards other early influences on the Baadshah's mind—and in this context the role of his tutors seems noteworthy. Two of them were Irani Shias—Bairam Khan and Mir Abdul Latif Qazvini—and the third was a Sunni Turani, Munim Khan. Luckily, all of them were above sectarian prejudices. In fact, if one digs deeper, beyond the general liberality of Akbar's immediate ancestors one finds the roots of toleration in the Mongol traditions. The cultural ethos of the Timurids promoted broad-mindedness. Timur respected all religions and Shias were never persecuted in the Timurid principalities. The *Yasa-i Chingezi* was literally a guidebook of the Timurids and according to Alauddin 'Ata Juwaini, it required the ruler 'to consider all sects as one and not to distinguish them from one another.' According to Juwaini, Chengiz Khan refrained from bigotry, communal preferences and discriminatory policies. In fact, Iqtidar Alam Khan attributes Akbar's persecution of the Shias and Mahdavis (1560) to the erosion of the influence of *Yasa-i-Chingezi*.[133]

In the 1560s, the Chishti Khanqahs (hospices) had introduced Akbar to a liberal way of thinking. In addition to his regard for Khwaja Muinuddin Chishti of Ajmer (d. 1236), he was particularly indebted to Shaikh Salim

---

[133]Ibid., pp. 155–56.

Chishti of Sikri (d. 1572). After the death of many of his newly born children, Akbar left one of his pregnant queens at the Shaikh's khanqah at Sikri and requested him to pray for the birth and survival of an heir. The prince born here lived and eventually succeeded Akbar as Jahangir, the fourth Mughal emperor. A massive palace complex and a lofty mosque were built at Sikri as a mark of the Baadshah's reverence. The Shaikh's majestic shrine was embellished with the finest marble lattice work possible, and the Buland Darwaza further added to the allure of the place. Akbar lovingly called his son, Shaikhu Baba. His other name was Salim, also after the Shaikh of Sikri, whose prayers were held to be instrumental in the prince's birth and survival. Shaikh Muhammad Ghaos and his son Shaikh Muhammad Ziyauddin were also consulted by the Baadshah for guidance. He was introduced to the ideas of Fana (an inexplicable state of existence in non-existence) and Wahdat ul wujud (unity of existence). In 1573, he regarded Khwaja Muinuddin Chishti as his spiritual preceptor and swore to kill anyone who said that the saint was 'gumrah' (misguided/lost). After 1575, he tried to learn the Chilla-i Ma 'kus (concentrating on God while suspended head down in a well for forty days and nights) from Shaikh Chaya Laddha (1575).[134] Badaoni reports that the Emperor took interest in learning various spiritual practices (1577).

While the Sufis pulled him towards liberality and humanism, Shaikh Mubarak and his sons Faizi and Abul

---

[134]Ibid., pp. 161–62.

Fazl (the author of the *Akbarnama/Ain-i Akbari*) assisted the Emperor in the ultimate fine-tuning of his secular inclinations. The idea of justifying taxes as wages of sovereignty, in a manner similar to the European Theory of Social Contract, was a sociopolitical stance framed by them. The Mughal theory of kingship thus formulated rested on the belief that if God did not withhold His bounty from anyone, how could the king, who was Zill-i Ilahi—just His shadow—discriminate? Irfan Habib says that there are two variants of Abul Fazl's theory of state with respect to the patronizing of secular governance and the creation of an intellectually integrated nobility. These variants, according to him, can be traced to heterodox tendencies in medieval Islam, prominent among them being Wahdat ul-wajud (Unity of Existence) of Ibn 'Arabi (1181–35) and the Farr-i Izadi (the Divine Light) of Shihab al-Din Suhrawardi Maqtul (d. 1191): the Sun shines for everybody, and that is how the king's bounty should be—undiscriminating. Iqtidar Alam Khan cites Habib:

> The influence of the pantheistic sufic doctrine of fana seems to have provided an impetus to Akbar's interest in philosophy. In the company of Sheikh Mubarak, Abul Fazl, Ghazi Khan Badakhshi, Hakim Abul Fath, and other rationalist thinkers, during 1578–82, he eventually became familiar with the systematic exposition of the doctrine of wahdat ul-wujud by Ibn al-'Arabi in a larger philosophical perspective. As Irfan Habib points out, the pantheism of Ibn al-'Arabi, despite lacking a rational basis, was

capable of becoming a strong ideological challenge to the post-Ghazali conventionalism in Islam. It was this quality of the impact of al-'Arabi's ideas on Akbar and, more importantly, on his socio-political perceptions during 1578–82, that is characterized by Abul Fazl as the elevation of 'intellect' (khirad) to a 'high pedestal' (buland paigi). The idea suggested by Ibn al-'Arabi that all that is not a part of divine reality is an illusion, in turn, led Akbar to the notion that all religions are either equally true or equally illusory, a suggestion that was bound to be sharply denounced by all shades of orthodox opinion as a deviation from the true path. It was equally unacceptable to the Jesuit fathers then present at the court. Commenting on Akbar's assurance in 1581 to Jalala Roshani of the freedom to practice his cult, Montserrat observed: 'the king cared little that in allowing everyone to follow his religion he was in reality violating all.[135]

◆

Rajputs and the Mughals: Unlearning Otherness

The Kachwahas of Ajmer had joined Akbar in 1561, and this saw the beginning of liberal policies towards the Rajputs. Chittor fell in 1567 and within three years of that most royal houses of Rajputana, except the Sisodias, joined the Mughal nobility. The following ten years

---

[135]Ibid., p. 162.

witnessed a rapid and remarkable rise in their power. Akbar's marriages with the daughters and nieces of the Rajput chieftains influenced him personally. For example, Abul Fazl reports that both at home and on travels, Akbar drank the water of the Ganges (the river and its water is considered sacred by the Hindus). It was brought for him in sealed jars. Food might have been cooked in rainwater or water from the Yamuna or the Chenab, but a bit of Ganga water was definitely mixed with it. The Abdaar Khana was the department in charge of looking into the water supply for the royal household.[136]

Badaoni, who was dismayed by the Baadshah's close connection with all religions and specially Hinduism, reports:

> The Samanas (Buddhist ascetics) and Brahmans brought forward proofs, based on reason and traditional testimony, for the truth of their own... His majesty firmly believed in the truth of the Christian religion, and wishing to spread the doctrines of Jesus ordered Prince Murad to take a few lessons in Christianity under good auspices, and charged Abu-l-Fazl to change the Gospel... Every day he (Akbar) used to put on clothes of that particular colour which accords with that of the regent-planet of the day. He began also, at midnight and early dawn to mutter the spells, which Hindus taught him, for the purpose of subduing the sun to his wishes. He

---

[136]Abraham Eraly, *The Mughal World Life in India's Last Golden Age*, Penguin Books India, New Delhi, 2007, p. 67.

prohibited the slaughter of cows and the eating of their flesh, because the Hindus devoutly worshipped them, and esteemed their dung as pure... This reason was also assigned, that physicians have represented that the flesh of cows to be productive of sundry kind of illnesses, and to be difficult of digestion. Fire worshippers also came from Nousari in Gujarat, proclaimed the religion of Zardusht as the true one and declared reverence to fire to be superior to every other kind of worship. They also attracted the emperor's regard, and taught him the peculiar terms, the ordinances, the rites and the ceremonies of the Kaiaanians(an old Persian dynasty). At last he ordered that the sacred fire should be made over to the charge of Abu-l-Fazl, and that after the manner of the kings of Persia, in whose temples blazed perpetual fires, he should take care it was never extinguished night or day, for that it is one of the signs of God, and one light from his lights... From early youth, in compliment to his wives, the daughters of the Rajahs of Hind, he had within the female apartments continued to offer the *hom*, which is a ceremony derived from sun-worship... On the festival of the eighth day after the Sun entering the Virgo in this year he came forth to the public-audience chamber with his forehead marked like a Hindu, and he had jewelled strings tied on his wrists by Brahmins, by way of a blessing. The chief and the nobles adopted the same practice in imitation of him, and presented on that day pearls and precious stones suitable to their respective wealth and station. It became the current custom also to wear the *rak'hi* on the wrist, which means an amulet formed out of twisted linen rags. Every precept which was enjoined by the doctors of other religions he treated as manifest and decisive, in contradiction to this religion of ours (Islam)...[137]

Badaoni writes that Akbar took such interest in understanding Hindu beliefs that priests sat on charpais (cots) which were suspended outside his personal bedchamber, and their discourse went on till late in the night. Badaoni says that the popularity of Hinduism among his subjects made him particularly soft towards it—'His majesty on hearing further how much the people of the country prized their institutions began to look upon them with affection.'[138]

According to him, the Emperor's supposed alienation from Muslim orthodoxy stemmed from the irreconcilable differences between the various schools of Islamic jurisprudence. Their refutation of each other led the emperor to doubt all of them. He says that when Akbar came to know of the worthlessness of the theologians of his own time, he inferred the unknown from the known and rejected their predecessors as well. He reports:

> There he used to spend much time in the Ibadat Khana in the company of learned men and Shaikhs. And specially on Friday nights when he would sit up there the whole night continually occupied in discussing

---

[137] Abdul Qadir Badaoni, *Muntakhab-ut Tawarikh*, Vol. II, G.S.A. Ranking (translation), Saeed International, New Delhi, 1990, pp. 264–69.
[138] Ibid., p. 265.

questions of religion, whether fundamental or collateral. The learned men used to draw the sword of the tongue on the battlefield of mutual contradiction and opposition, and the antagonism of the sects reached such a pitch that they would call one another heretics and fools.[139]

To explain the rise of Abul Fazl in the Mughal court, Badaoni says that the patronization came because in Fazl, Akbar saw someone capable enough to teach a lesson to the Mullas (orthodox Muslim clerics)—whose arrogance, Badaoni mocks, was like that of the Pharaoh (the ruler of Egypt renowned for his relentless pride, who was in conflict with Moses). In this regard, Shireen Moosvi cites the *Muntakhab-ut Tawarikh* as follows:

> ...[T]ill one night the vein of the neck of the Ulama of the age swelled up, and there were loud voices and tumult. His majesty got very angry at this behaviour and said to me, 'in future report any of these people whom you find talking nonsense, and I shall expel him from the assembly.' I said in low tones to Asaf Khan, 'If I carried out this order, most of the Ulama would have to be expelled.' His Majesty asked what I had said. I conveyed to His majesty what I had actually said. He was highly pleased, and mentioned my remark to those sitting near him. He used to summon Makhdumu'l Mulk Maulana Abdullah Sultanpuri to that assembly, in order to annoy him, and would set up to argue

---

[139]Ibid., pp. 267 and 262.

against him Hajji Ibrahim and Shaikh Abu'l Fazl, then a new arrival, but now a prime leader of the New Religion and Faith, or rather the Infallible Guide and Representative with full powers with several other new comers.[140]

Abul Fazl records the Baadshah saying that a true mystic guide is the one who recognizes the sorrows and anxieties of his followers and guides them towards a solution, so that they may be relieved of stress. Only maintaining some stereotypical appearance was hardly the signature of a master of spirituality. The lack of Sulh-i kul had caused avoidable disharmony in Hindustan.

In an effort to understand Hinduism and popularize its understanding in the Persian speaking world, Akbar established a Maktab Khana (translation bureau) and ordered the translation of many Sanskrit works. Some examples are the *Singhasan Battisi* (*Nama-i Khirad Afza*), *Atharva Veda* (*Atharban*), *Mahabharata* (*Razm-nama*), *Ramayana*, *Harivansha Purana* (*Haribans*), *Lilavati* (Bhasrakacharya's work on Arithmetic dated 1150), *Tajikanilkanthi* (*Tajik*; a work on astronomy), *Rajtarangini* (Kalhana's famous history of Kashmir) and *Panchatantra* (animal tales with lessons on wisdom). The *Iyar-i Danish* was inspired by the *Panchatantra* and Faizi's *Nal Daman* was a retelling of an indigenous tale in Persian.[141]

Mirza Abdu'r Rahim Khan-i Khanan (one of Akbar's

---

[140]*Episodes in the Life of Akbar*, pp. 63–4.
[141]M. Athar Ali, *Mughal India Studies in Polity, Ideas, Society and Culture*, Oxford University Press, New Delhi, 2006, pp. 173–81.

closest associates) had commissioned the Persian translation of the Arabic *Mirror of Princes*, entitled *Siraajul Muluk* (1122), written by a Spanish author, Abu Bakr Muhammad bin al-Walid Turtushi (d. 1127). Athar Abbas Rizvi opines that this translation served to encourage the political theorists of Akbar's times to refer to varied sources, as Turtushi had done. Scholars of Iran, Byzantium, China, Hind and Sind were cited by him. His work drew inspiration from the *Kalila wa dimma* and refers to *Muntakhab al Jawahir* (*Selected Gems*), composed by the Indian Shanaq (Chanakya), as a guide for the monarchs. This text, the *Kitaab Shaanaq fi al-tadbir*, was the celebrated *Chanakyaniti*—a collection of political aphorisms in Sanskrit (not to be confused with the *Arthashastra* ascribed to Kautilya or Chanakya).[142]

As noted by Irfan Habib, Abul Fazl opined that Indian culture was not studied by the Muslims because there had been no freedom of enquiry under the burden of inherited tradition. 'The path of asking how and why had been closed.' During Akbar's reign, reason was glorified and the doors of questioning and inquiry were reopened. The concluding part of the *Ain-i Akbari* has a chapter on India's religions, thoughts and customs. It is remarkable that it rests on the idea of India as a unit of culture of which Muslims were as much a part as were Hindus, Jains and Buddhists. This, Habib emphasizes, is the first explicit and consistent treatment of Indian culture as a composite one.[143] The

---

[142]Cf. *Akbar And His Age*, pp. 16–17.
[143]*Akbar And His Age*, p. xv.

translation project aimed at lessening the social distances. It was not about power or politics—it was about people.

◆

A Baadshah Cured of Depression

Reports suggest that Akbar used to have occasional fits of depression and melancholy at least up till 1578. Antonio Montserrat, a contemporary, observed that the king had a somewhat morose disposition. The psychological dips might have been the manifestation of some neurotic disorder, but are explained by Abul Fazl and Akbar himself as spiritual experiences.[144] Perhaps his separation from his parents during infancy and the subsequent stay with uncles who were hostile towards his father could have triggered this kind of a psyche. Before 1578, the monarch had a tendency to take life-threatening risks. For example, he had once endangered his life by mounting an untamable elephant (1561). Shireen Moosvi's adaptation of the event from the *Akbarnama* reads as follows:

> Among the occurrences of this time was His Majesty the Emperor's mounting the elephant Hawai and engaging it in a fight. The elephant Hawai was a mighty animal and belonged to the Imperial stables. In rapid pace, proneness to anger, fierceness and wickedness he was a match for the world. Expert and experienced drivers, who had spent a long life in riding similar

---

[144]*India's Polity in the Age of Akbar*, p. 157.

elephants, mounted him with difficulty, so what could they do in the way of making him fight? The heroic and brave Emperor one day without hesitation mounted this elephant, in the very height of his musth and excitement, in the polo-ground which he had made for his pleasure, outside the fort of Agra, and executed wonderful manoeuvres. After that he pitted him against the elephant Ran Bagha which nearly approached him in his qualities. The loyal and the experienced who were present were in a state such as should never happen to anyone.

As the courtiers who were witnesses of this dangerous scene were agitated by its prolongation and were unable to remonstrate, they in their desperation thought that there might be a remedy if Atka Khan, who was the main minister at the Court, was brought, and if he, by prayers and entreaties could dissuade His Majesty from pursuing this dreadful occupation, the contemplation of which turned the gall bladder of the iron-hearted to water. When Atka Khan arrived in all distraction and saw the state of affairs, he dropped from his hand the thread of self-control and bared his head. He cried and lamented like oppressed suppliants for justice. Great and small raised hands of entreaty and implored God for the safety of the sacred person, the fountainhead of peace and tranquility for mankind. When his Majesty chanced to see Atka Khan's perturbation, he said to him, 'you must not make all this lamentation. If you don't stop, I'll at once throw myself down from the elephant.' When

Atka Khan saw His Majesty's firm determination in the business, he at once obeyed and from deference outwardly composed his internal agitation.[145]

This incident was not a random one. On many occasions, as in elephant fights or hunts, he had consciously imperilled his life. The last of his unexplained seizures came in the midst of a hunting expedition (1578). Akbar had fainted and Abul Fazl records that it was feared that he would not survive this one. But he did, and this time, bounced back to master his nerves like never before. It is after 1578 that his policy of Sulh-i kul takes a definite shape—and probably the first relationship that it healed was that of the king with himself.

It is well proven that Akbar had a tendency to experiment and search for rational answers. For example, a male deer was mated with a Barbari goat as an experiment ordered by him, and a non-productive hybrid deer was born out of the cross-breeding. His experimentations based on the idea of Zabaan-i Qudrat (natural tongue/dialect) was more intriguing. Some newly-born infants were isolated in a palace called the Gung Mahal (palace of the dumb) and were raised in a speechless environment. Their caretakers were not allowed to utter a single word in their presence. On their own, the children did not develop any mode of verbal communication, proving the notion that hearing is a key factor in speaking (1579–1580).[146] Badaoni reports

---

[145] *Episodes in the Life of Akbar*, pp. 23–4.
[146] *Episodes in the Life of Akbar*, pp. 90–91 and *India's polity in the age of Akbar*, p. 158.

that 'Questions of Sufism, scientific discussions, enquiries into Philosophy and Law were the order of the day.'[147] It is thus no wonder that, ultimately, there was an insistence on 'aql' (reason) over 'taqlid' (reflex/ imitation/dogmatism). Ritualism was discouraged and rationalism was encouraged. The Baadshah argued that if blind following of traditions was all that commendable, then prophets would have only followed their predecessors instead of preaching anything reformative. The following extract, from Shireen Moosvi's translation of the *Akbarnama*, is Akbar's reply to his son Murad's query regarding officials who practised jismaniat (physical exercises) as rituals of worship:

> Multiplicity of groups of people is a manifestation of divine power. That which is dictated by the principles of reason and suits the circumstances of the rulers and managers of affairs of the multitude is that they should practice 'Absolute Peace' (Sulh-i kul) with the entire world and mankind. Wishing well and admonishing is excellent in the case of every person. Everyone who comes to the path of reason may be fortunate. And every one who remains miserable in the barren land of tradition is an invalid. Every person recognizing and worshipping God in whatever way is (however) welcome. Preventing that insensitive simpleton, who considers body exercise to be divine worship, from (practicing) this form of worship would amount to preventing him from remembering God (at all).[148]

---

[147]*Muntakhab-ut Tawarikh*, p. 203.
[148]*Episodes in the Life of Akbar*, p. 95 and *India's polity in the age of*

Iqtidar Alam Khan opines that Akbar's eagerness to conform to an accepted code of ethical and legal behaviour was a trait which he had inherited from his father.[149] Montserrat records:

> [The] King's severity towards errors and misdemeanours committed by officers in the course of government business is remarkable, for he is most stern with offenders against the public faith ...for the King has the most precise regard for right and justice in the affairs of government...by the King's direction all capital cases, and all really important civil cases also, are conducted before himself. He is easily excited to anger, but soon cools down again. By nature moreover he is kindly and benevolent, and is sincerely anxious that guilt should be punished, without malice indeed, but at the same time without undue leniency.[150]

Although Akbar could never have matched the literary education of his immediate ancestors he was always interested in classics like the *Masnawi* of Maulana Jalaluddin Rumi (d. 1273) and the *Diwan* of Hafiz Shirazi (d. 1317). Abul Fazl reports that he recited extempore from these texts. Shireen Moosvi presents the following verse from the *Akbarnama* penned by the Emperor himself:

> This is not the chain of insanity on the neck of the afflicted Majnun.

Akbar, pp. 164–5.
[149] *India's Polity in the Age of Akbar*, p. 158.
[150] *The Mughal World*, p. 258.

It is the hand of affection that love has laid on his neck.[151]

◆

Ibadat Khana: Prescience of an Awakening

In the pre-1571 phase, Akbar had ordered the exhumation of the remains of Mir Murtaza Sharifi Shirazi from the vicinity of Amir Khusrau's tomb in Delhi on the suggestion of Shaikh Abdun Nabi (1567). The argument given by the latter was that a 'heretic' could not be allowed to rest in the precincts of a venerable Sufi's shrine. His farman to Abdus Samad, the Muhtasib of Bilgram, to eradicate heresy (1572), and the suppression of Mahadavis in Gujarat (1573), indicated that he was under the influence of the orthodoxy. In fact, the Mahadavi saint Miyan Mustafa Bandagi was arrested.[152] Approximately from 1571 onwards, he was deeply influenced by the pantheistic Sufi doctrines. Pantheism is the belief that God is identifiable with the forces of nature and with natural substances, implying acceptance of many forms of divinity. This naturally conflicted with the traditional orthodoxy and institutionalized systems of religion.

Akbar found the Sukhan-i Hikmat (philosophical discourses) 'dil-awez' and 'dil-ruba' (enchanting);[153] the fact that post-Ghazali Islamic theologians discouraged it

---

[151]*Episodes in the Life of Akbar*, p. 97.
[152]*India's Polity in the Age of Akbar*, p. 160–61.
[153]Ibid., p. 159.

was hardly a matter of concern for him. Mystics argued that hope derived from God's mercy is a much better idea to bank upon than the notion of fear of His rage. Akbar believed that ascribing evil entirely to Satan is limiting the absoluteness of God, because everything is designed by Him, including evil. The real manifestation of the conflict with Iblis-Almuzzill (the devil/Satan the tempter) is the conflict with our own weaknesses and endless worldly desires.[154] It is not a conflict with people of other faiths, but with our own faithlessness. He said that most worshippers worship because they wish for the fulfilment of some desire. They are not devoted out of pure adoration of the divine. The demon is within us, and so the combat has to be contained there.

In the Ibadat Khana discussions organized under his aegis, experts of various faiths were invited to present their views. The king tried to discover the parallel lines of argument and the common denominator in different religions. Besides the intra-Muslim debates on Islamic theology and jurisprudence, inter-religious discussions also took place. He realized soon enough that rituals hindered the formulation of common modalities of life for people; they divided them. Perhaps that is why 'formality' received a royal dressing-down by Sulh-i kul. The biggest take away from these discussions was the idea that a Sultan-i Adil (Just King) was above the Mujtahid (authorities on Islamic laws who are competent enough to make independent judgements/interpretations). This gave

---

[154]*Mughal India*, p. 161.

the Baadshah an advantage over the Muslim orthodoxy, and he used it to pave the way for exceptionally liberal policies. The idea of the supremacy of the king's discretion in all religious matters was codified in a legal document duly attested by witnesses—the *Mahzar* (1579). It declared that Akbar was the Sultan-i Islam and his rulings would be binding on everyone, provided that his orders were not contrary to the explicit injunctions of the Quran. According to Syed Athar Abbas Rizvi, these powers were moulded in the matrix of the political philosophy of Imam Ghazai (1058–1111) and his contemporary, Nizamul Mulk Tusi (1018–1092), and could not be questioned by authorities on Muslim jurisprudence.[155] It was an experiment considered extremely dangerous by Muslim traditionalists. Their apprehension that the king wanted a share in their slice of power unnerved them. The nobility, which was already annoyed due to Akbar's insistence on Daagh-o Chehra, found this an opportune time to rise in revolt.

It seemed that the experiment had failed—but it hadn't. The so called 'failure' of the *Mahzar* made Akbar realize once and for all that belonging to a particular religion does not bind people in any way except nominally. It is their take on everyday ethics like loyalty, commitment and humanism that can categorize people as dependable or otherwise. Therefore, Madad-i-Maash land grants given to the Muslim ulema were curtailed and revolts were crushed with an iron hand. It became clear that Akbar was heading

---

[155] *Akbar and His Age*, p. 11.

towards a secular, religion-neutral state. The supposedly failed experiment had in fact changed the game.

◆

Sulh-i kul: The Pacific Calm

Sulh-i kul's homophonic/polyphonic character was so pronounced that Akbar believed that either all faiths are true or all are untrue. He professed that rituals created illusions of differences between religions, and they are redundant. Therefore outward show of religiosity should be shunned and God should be perceived from a mystical point of view rather than a ritualistic one. 'Din' (faith/formalism) is as illusionary as 'duniya' (the world).

In the *Ain-i Akbari,* Abul Fazl says Akbar had articulated that pursuit of virtue should neither be motivated by the ideas of death and temporariness of the world, nor by fear or hope. No justification is required for practising morality, integrity, fairness, kindness etc. One should be virtuous because it is good to be so. Much ahead of his times, he opined that being sincere towards one's profession was also a form of worship. He said, 'Let the peshawar (professionals) be more skilled at their work and that is divine worship for them.'[156] No wonder Badaoni wrote, 'From childhood to manhood and from manhood to his declining years the Emperor (Akbar) had combined in himself various phases from various religions and opposite

---

[156]*Episodes in the Life of Akbar*, p. 127–28.

sectarian beliefs, and by a peculiar acquisitiveness and a talent for selection, by no means common, had made his own all that can be seen and read in books'.[157]

Montserrat felt that when Akbar allowed everyone to practise their religion, he was in fact violating all of them. Formalism and divisive tendencies were criticized and Akbar came close to the Nirgun Bhakti sects that criticized all types of ritualism, Hindu catholicity as well as Muslim orthodoxy. Shaikh Ahmad Sarhindi tried to convince Jahangir that the 'weakness' of Akbar's time was that he had allowed everyone to practise their faith. In this context, Man Singh's reply to an offer to enrol himself in Akbar's spiritual club is rather interesting: 'If discipleship means willingness to sacrifice one's life, I have already carried my life in hand, what need is there of proof? If however, the term has another meaning and refers to faith, I certainly am a Hindu.'[158]

Luckily, Jahangir approved of his father's Sulh-i kul and proudly informed the readers of his autobiography, the *Tuzuk-i Jahangiri*, that the Shias and the Sunnis offered namaz in the same mosque in Akbar's times. Unlike other kingdoms of the world, the followers of various faiths had room in the broad expanse of his father's matchless empire. He noted that in Iran there was room only for Shiites alone and in Turkey, India and Turan there was room for only the Sunnis. However, just as in the wide expanse of Divine Compassion there is room for all classes and the followers

---

[157]*Muntakhab-ut Tawarikh*, p. 263.
[158]Ibid., p. 375.

of all creeds, so in his father's dominions, which were limited on all sides only by the salt sea, on the principle that the shadow must have the same properties as light there was room for the followers of opposite religions, and for beliefs right and wrong, and the road to altercation was closed. Sunnis and Shiites met in one mosque, and Franks and Jews in one church, and worshipped and prayed as they wished. He wrote that his father associated with the good of every race and creed and persuasion and was gracious to all in accordance with their condition and understanding. It is noteworthy that Jahangir records an anecdote regarding Shaikh Nizamuddin Auliya which promotes interfaith harmony: once, seated on the terrace of his Khanqah, the Shaikh watched Hindus proceeding towards the Yamuna for some ritual. When Amir Khusrau joined him, he asked whether Khusrau had noticed the crowd and remarked that each nation/race has its right road of faith and its shrine.

Jahangir's perception of Sulh-i kul is summed up in the following passage:

> They (those who follow him) are not to darken and disturb their time by enmity to any of the religious communities (*millat-a*) and with all persons of the various creeds they should pursue the path of Absolute Peace (Sulh-i kul). They should kill no living being with their own hands, nor should they skin anything except in war and chase… The lame, the ignorant, the sleepy-looking, the unmannerly; you (too) should go on looking at Him and calling Him. My father had

obtained mastery over these truths, and few were the times when he was free from such thoughts.[159]

Thus by neutralizing religion, Akbar tried to constitute a nobility which might be heterogeneous on apparent racial and religious parameters, but was homogenous intellectually. Religion was not used as a marker of differences, humanity was. Beyond a point he stopped bothering about a justification of his authority within the Muslim framework. If there was anything which was used to justify his majestic powers, it was his humanness.

It is noticeable that the shade of Sulh-i kul was so deep on the Mughal fabric that when Aurangzeb was soliciting support from Rana Raj Singh of Mewar in the course of the war of succession with his father and brothers, he referred to Akbar's policy of inclusion as bait. A precious document from Udaipur records the following words of Aurangzeb's nishan (princely order): 'God willing when the truth comes into its own and the wishes of the sincerely loyal ones are fulfilled (i.e. when Aurangzeb gains the throne), the benefits of the revered practices and established regulations of my great ancestors, who are so esteemed by the worshipful ones, will cast lustre on the four-cornered, inhabited world.'[160]

Besides insistence on secularism, Akbar's disapproval of gendered social practices can be noted in his discouragement of child marriages, widow immolation and the questioning of a lesser share for females in an

---

[159]*Mughal India*, pp. 164 and 186.
[160]Ibid., p. 246.

Islamic division of property. His empathy for the wife of a dak-chauki messenger is remarkable. Prince Murad had requested for the transfer of a particular dak-chauki messenger, Bahadur, to his station. However, Akbar replied that his wife was not presently keen on that posting for her husband, and hoped that eventually he may be able to persuade her.[161] The wishes of the wife of a humble dak-chauki messenger were valued. Indeed, the Baadshah was empathy personified!

He encouraged vegetarianism and said that one should not make one's stomach the grave of animals. Abul Fazl records that the vegetarian food was called 'Sufiyana' (mystical/chaste). Nizamuddin Ahmad reports that the Baadshah had ordered that a portion of the food cooked for him should first be served to the needy, and that he was so grateful for the food that he got to eat, he prostrated in thankfulness. He dressed rather simply. Although many clothes were stitched on his orders, most were used as presents to be given away.[162]

His insistence on fair dispensation of justice was impressive. The following stance in his own words is classic: 'If I were guilty of an unjust act, I would rise in judgment against myself. What shall I say then of my sons, my kindred and others.'[163] He feared that the medieval right to retaliation and bloody settlement of scores could become an uncontrollable menace, and the assassination of

---

[161] *India's Polity in the Age of Akbar*, p.165
[162] *The Mughal World*, p. 67.
[163] Ibid., 258.

Adham Khan by the Baadshah was meant to be a message to the nobility that even the closest of his allies would be punished for unlawful behaviour. Adham Khan was the son of Maham Anga, but Akbar's reverence for her didn't stop him from doing what had to be done. Abul Fazl reports that he didn't trust witnesses easily and searched carefully for contradictions in their narratives and physical signs of discomfiture. The judges were advised to make thorough enquiries before reaching any conclusion. The physiognomy of suspects and foresight was to be put to use. He abhorred torture. The punishment of criminals was to be staggered into reprimands followed by threats and then imprisonment. Mutilation was to be used only in very serious cases. The officers were always advised to give capital punishment with caution, but by 1582, he altogether prohibited the use of this punishment by officers, and this decree was followed by his successors. By and large the idea was to reform criminals by good counsel.[164]

It is extremely important to note that theologians like Shaikh Abdul Haq Muhaddis and Shaikh Nurul Haq prayed for Akbar as a Muslim ruler and opined that his motives were misunderstood by the common man. Syed Athar Abbas Rizvi asserts that: 'He (Akbar) had vowed only to liberate and disassociate himself (ibra wa tabarra namuda) from the traditional and imitative religion (din-i majazi wa taqlidi). There is no doubt that he did repudiate the taqlidi Islam but he was not hostile to Islam that found Sulh-i kul

---

[164]Ibid., pp. 264–65.

imperative to its body politic.'[165] Their assessment of the Baadshah is important because if true, it clearly implies that Akbar had understood that he doesn't have to be an atheist to respect all religions. He cautioned against those rituals of every religion which conflated religiosity and humanism. A true follower of any religion—any religion at all—is certain to have humanism as his basic nature. Once that position is taken, respect for other religions and the variety of creation would follow with the involuntariness of a beating heart.

---

[165]Cf. *Akbar and His Age*, p. 20.

Conclusion

Looking Back, and the Omnipresent Past

Grateful are the Grateful
Happy are the Happy
Human are the Humane.

The fact that words like 'ended', 'late', 'former', 'gone', 'bygone', 'dead' and 'dead and buried', are suggested as synonyms for 'past' is an enigma wrapped in mystery. The mix-up can be explained by the contradiction that the past is the most everlasting thing. It is living and constantly growing. Each passing second adds to its immeasurable volume. The present speeds towards the future, but both are eventually overtaken by the past. Thus all future is would-be past, and in this sense they are close-knit ideas.

It is sometimes suggested that a study of the past facilitates the prediction of the future. In this sense, what has happened brings us closer to what is going to happen. However to get a handle on such predications can be as baffling as crystal-gazing. Both the excess and the scarcity of historical data make it difficult. A further roadblock is popped by varied interpretations of the data by earlier searchers. Some of these interpretations themselves become data with the passage of time. Thus a rambler has to understand that a passage through history is more of an acrobatic walk on a tightrope between truths and lies. Episodes have to be evened out by trends; however, some of them dynamically dissent from strong tendencies. It is for the historian to catch the drift with exactitude and tilt in the right direction. Further, to understand the mind of authors and data collectors is also a tricky task. Historians try to peel off the mask that the authors of their sources wear. Corroboration with other sources and a general overview of the times help in understanding the agendas of authors, yet all camouflage is not penetrable. If we are to assume that the past is a tapestry of colourful diamonds, a close scrutiny may reveal that some of them were stolen and replaced with fakes. Tracking thieves of truth is a difficult task, but consciously holding on to one's own objectivity and integrity is equally challenging.

Following are excerpts from interviews of stalwart historians of our times. The two questions posed to them were: What are the thing/things that they have learnt from History and found valuable in a personal sense, and if they were to narrate an event/events/episode/episodes from History which they think could bring peace/happiness/wisdom to humans, what would it/they be?

Satish Chandra

During my student days at the Allahabad University I learnt that nationalism could be a powerful phenomenon.

However, nationalism can also have types. The nationalism which I learnt of in my student days is now called secularism. For me secularism was nationalism. As students and individuals we did not view the Turks and the Mughals as blights. The reason for this was that we looked at the negatives and the positives of everything. My close association with Prof. Saiyid Nurul Hasan and Prof. Mohammad Habib taught me to not look at History and the world through a keyhole, but to look at the big picture and to never judge people and things in absolute black and white. The other thing which needs to be emphasized is that History is a very changeable thing although it might appear totally factual and static. A thing that we once thought was positive may become negative after the passage of some time. So as time passes events might get 'evened out' on their own due to change in perspectives. Therefore we must seek History with neutrality and not seek it with a preconditioned mindset of negatives or positives, or an agenda that we would present a certain persona or phase as positive or negative. If we take the revolt of 1857, before 1947, the event was studied with comparative neutrality. Some people were looking at and highlighting its positives and some others were highlighting its negatives. But after 1947 we predominantly sung of and hung on to the positives only. Incidentally, one of the greatest positives of the revolt was recognized much later, and it was that the feudal ruling class, which had dominated the political scene directly or indirectly and of course was highly exploitative, was finally pushed to the margins of the political picture and a new nationalist type of force grew, which eventually gained much strength in the future.

As far as learning from History is concerned, one of the greatest achievements which should be highlighted is Akbar's attitude of Sulh-i-kul. It was a firm foundation of peace and happiness. His idea of associating closely with the Rajputs was a great move not only in the context of diplomacy of the times but that of acceptance of the Other. I have divided this alliance into three phases. First, when the Rajputs were inducted as warriors. Second, when they became partners of the Mughals and the sword arm of the empire. This attitude persisted till the time of Aurangzeb, who tried his best to befriend them in the initial phase of his reign. However, after the death of Jai Singh and Jaswant Singh, his attitude changed. The third phase is marked by the beginning of the process of distancing, which ultimately matured into an almost negative attitude.

The second thing which I think needs to be essentially highlighted is the Bhakti Movement, and within that the dialogue between the Nirgun Bhakti trends and Islam. The liberals of all religions interacted very closely with each other in the course of this movement. They recognized that everything is a combination of positives and negatives. What is important is what dominates. When we talk of recognizing domination, it should not be limited to finding the positives and negatives in events; it is also about recognizing the positives and negatives inside our own head and to consciously let the positive dominate.

Harbans Mukhia

It is hard to pinpoint one thing one learns from History; there are several lessons we imbibe both in our personal life as well as our understanding of the world around. The one big lesson History bestows upon us is how societies undergo drastic change over time and yet how old structures of political power, of social and cultural norms, of mindscapes retard the all-encompassing change. Every age, indeed every moment is thus a moment of tension between continuity and change where the two often go hand in hand. There is, in other words, much change in continuity and much continuity in change. Greek philosopher Heraclitus (sixth–fifth century BC) had sharply counter-posed continuity and change in asserting 'you can never put your hand in the same river twice.' However, he failed to notice that even as the water in which you put your hand a moment ago has flowed away, the river still remains.

One has thus seen the world and humanity undergo humongous changes in every sphere: technology, economy, society, ecology, religions, political ideologies, feudalism, capitalism, socialism, absolutism, democracy, human rights...the list is unending. Several of these have come and gone, several others have remained alive. Above all, certain human cravings: for peace and love and for violence and war.

A crucial agency of change has been and still remains the State. In the midst of State-Society interaction, the State remains the driver of change even in the arena of religion. Buddhism, Hinduism, Christianity, Islam—all spread under the aegis of the State. Political, administrative, economic structures evolved under its aegis too. On the other hand, all of these religions—and for that matter, the whole spectrum of religious or secular ideologies and cultures—arose at the ground level and gained momentum, sometimes in the form of social movements, and at others as movements against the currently established political and social regimes. It is thus that understanding the society of the present or the past can never be a simplistic either/or quest. It is always way too complex to be subject to sheer reduction.

At a personal level, History has taught me patience with change around me. And the enormous range of human achievements through history in all societies has left me with great admiration for the plurality of cultures around the world without either grandstanding any one culture or the slightest touch of animosity towards others. There should be acceptance, appreciation and admiration rather than mere tolerance. I love to be part of all of them by being part of one.

Let me first invert the question and go back to one major event in my life (or perhaps the lives of those of us who come from the pre-1947 era): The one event that has brought extreme suffering to humans and what does it tell us about avoidance of it? Of course wars between states have brought untold and incomparable suffering through human history and continue to do so. But the one great event I am talking about here is not war between states but conflict between 'societies': the Partition of India in

1947. In some ways the events that followed in the wake of the Partition brought home the ugliest face of nationalism. Whether we accept the two-nation theory or not, the ground reality brought the 'two nations' into their most brutal, most horrendous manifestation of inhumanity vis-à-vis ones who had been their neighbours and friends and co-workers in the fields and factories and offices for decades, even centuries; one with whom the relations were the most cordial. Rabindranath Tagore was ideologically hostile to the very idea of nationalism, which for him signified dominance and subjugation of one segment of humanity by another. He visualized nationalism and humanism as one another's negation. He was in some ways fortunate to have died before he could witness the rivers of human bloodshed by fellow humans who had for long, very long, been friends; for the establishment of two independent nations. But the rivers of blood in 1947 also hid any number of humane acts of life saving kindness and help extended to one-another, if under the shadows of terror. Several graphic accounts of these acts have been unearthed and recorded, most recently by Professor Ishtiaq Ahmed of Stockholm University in his brilliant book, *The Punjab: Bloodied, Partitioned and Cleansed*. My own immediate family also happens to have been a recipient of such kindness and help at grave risk to the help giver. What lesson does this 'event' yield to us about peace/happiness for humans? That if humanity and humanism is the one value that both precedes and supersedes all ideological formations—religions, nationalism, socialism etc.—it is also the most fragile and fractures at the first sight of an adversarial assault. It is therefore all the more important for our happiness and peace to lend it all our strength.

Dwijendra Narayan Jha

There should be no place for religious fundamentalism. It divides people. A critical analysis of the past enables me to take a stand on contemporary issues whose roots go back in time.

Iqtidar Husain Siddiqui

There are numerous examples in History when people didn't give up. They kept trying to achieve what they believed in and fought for their convictions. Razia Sultan and Sher Shah Suri are examples of unbeatable resilience. It is never too late to learn new things. Afghans acquired many skills and trades they were not conventionally involved in.

Shireen Moosvi

If India has had a history, unfortunately, of religious dogma and intolerance, it has also a contrary tradition of religious coexistence. Aśoká's Rock Edict XII of over 2,250 years ago can still resonate with us just as Akbar's religious tolerance seems to have a contemporary ring. In his *Hind Swaraj*, Gandhiji declared with absolute clarity that the nation had nothing to do with religion, and so he called on people of all religions in India 'to live in unity'. Secularism is, therefore, an irremovable pillar of our nationhood. Any weakening of secularism by divisive forces, which have grown so strong today, will endanger the very bonds that tie our nation together.

India grew into a nation in the course of its struggle for independence. Contrary to the idea promoted by communalists of the day that India suffered eight hundred years of 'foreign rule', the fact is that the rule of one country over another, whereby part of the wealth and income of the subject territory is transferred forcibly to the ruling one and its markets are similarly seized by the other, is a modern phenomenon linked to the rise of colonialism—beginning with Columbus and Vasco da Gama at the end of the fifteenth century. In India it began recognizably with Plassey (1757). Resistance in the governed country remain local or regional, as it was in India even in 1857—when more than half the country continued to be unaffected. Here it was mainly the increasing realization of the consciousness of being exploited that played a radical role in the making of a subject country into a nation, emerging as a radical counterpart of what Benedict Anderson calls the 'official nationalism' of the imperialist countries.

As the National Movement grew, the struggle for equitable society became a part of Gandhiji's own Constructive Programme of 1920s, and, at a fairly radical level, was reflected in the Congress's Karachi Resolution on Fundamental Rights, 1931, drafted by Jawaharlal Nehru and moved formally by Gandhiji.

An Indian nation was thus created, in which all classes of people could feel that they had a share. It was created not only in opposition to the British rulers, but also in face of hostility from within, especially from the advocates of the 'two-nation' theory—based on religious identities—headed by Vir Savarkar and M.A. Jinnah. Partition was the price paid. But in what remained of India, a dream was widely shared, one that moved Jawaharlal Nehru as well as his critics—a dream that India would stand as a secular, democratic and socialist republic. We hope that the people of India will protect the essence of what we have inherited and what humanistic values we wish to add to that inheritance.

◆

Of course, experiments and personal experiences are great teachers too. Quite like the front view. However, we need to balance the rear and the front view to drive safely. The omnipresence of the past is unstoppable, but we might try to restrict its omnipotence, specially in matters where its negative influence may damage the fabric of humanness. When you fight wars on the side of humanism, there are no defeats. The kind of victories might not be predictable, but they are guaranteed.

Bibliography

Abbas Khan Sarwani, *Tarikh-i Sher Shahi*, Vol-II, S.M. Imam al-Din (edited and translated), University of Dacca, Dacca, 1964.

Abdul Qadir Badaoni, *Muntakhab-ut Tawarikh*, Vols-I and II, G.S.A. Ranking (translation), Saeed International/Atlantic Publishers and Distributors, New Delhi, 1990.

Abraham Eraly, *The Mughal World Life in India's Last Golden Age*, Penguin Books India, New Delhi, 2007.

Ashvini Agrawal, *Rise and Fall of the Imperial Guptas*, Motilal Banarasidass, Delhi, 1989.

Clayton M. Christensen, James Allworth, Karen Dillon, *How Will You Measure Your Life*, HarperCollins Publishers, London, 2012.

D.C. Sircar, *Landlordism and Tenancy in Ancient and Early Medieval India as Revealed by Epigraphical Records*, University of Lucknow, Lucknow, 1969.

Fatima Hussain, *The War that Wasn't: The Sufi and the Sultan*, Munshiram Manoharlal, New Delhi, 2009.

Firdausi, *Shahnama, The Shah Nameh of the Persian Poet Firdausi*, James Atkinson (translated and abridged), Rev. J.A. Atkinson (edited), Frederick Warne and Co., London, 1886.

H.C. Roychoudhuri, *A Political History of Ancient India: From the*

Accession of Parikshit to the Extinction of the Gupta Dynasty, University of Calcutta, Calcutta, 1923.

Iqtidar Alam Khan (edited), *Akbar and His Age*, Northern Book Centre, New Delhi, 1999.

Iqtidar Alam Khan, *India's Polity in the Age of Akbar*, Permanent Black, and Ashoka University, Ranikhet, 2016.

Iqtidar Husain Siddiqui, *Authority and Kingship under the Sultans of Delhi*, Manohar, New Delhi, 2006.

Iqtidar Husain Siddiqui, *Composite Culture under the Sultanate of Delhi*, Primus Books, Delhi, 2012.

Irfan Habib, *The Agrarian System of Mughal India 1556–1707*, Second Revised Edition, Oxford University Press, 1999.

Jouher Aftabchi, *Tazkirat-ul Waqiat*, translation Major Charles Stewart, Idarah-i Adabiyat-i Delli, Delhi, 1972.

Meena Bhargava (edited), *Exploring Medieval India: Sixteenth to Eighteenth Centuries*, Vol-II, Orient BlackSwan, New Delhi, 2010.

Mohammad Athar Ali, *Mughal India Studies in Polity, Ideas, Society and Culture*, Oxford University Press, New Delhi, 2006

Romila Thapar, *Somanatha: The Many Voices of a History*, Penguin Viking, New Delhi, 2004.

Rummer Godden, *Gulbadan: Portrait of a Rose Princess at the Mughal Court*, The Viking Press, New York, 1980.

Sadi Shirazi, *Bustan*, cf. *The Bustan of Sadi*, A. Hart Edwards, Kitab Bhavan, New Delhi, 2000.

Satish Chandra, *Medieval India from Sultanate to the Mughals*, Part-I, Har-Anand Publications, Pvt. Ltd. New Delhi, 2001.

Shaikh Rizqullah Mushtaqui, *Waqiat-i Mushtaqi*, Iqtidar Husain Siddiqui (translated and edited), Indian Council of Historical Research and Northern Book Centre, New Delhi, 1992.

Shireen Moosvi, *Episodes in the Life of Akbar*, National Book Trust, New Delhi, 1994.

Singhasan Battisi, Lalluji Lal Kabi (translation from Sanskrit to Hindi), Syed Abdoollah (revised & corrected with copious notes), W.H. Allen & Co, London, 1869.

Upinder Singh, *A History of Ancient and Early Medieval India: From the Stone Age to the 12th Century*, Pearson, New Delhi, 2009.

Ziauddin Barani, *Tarikh-i Firoz Shahi*, Ishtiyaq Ahmad Zilli (translation), Primus Books, Delhi, 2015.

Index

Abbas Khan Sarwani, 131–32, 134–45
Abdul Qadir Badaoni, 3, 18, 28, 35, 159
Abdul Qasim Firdausi, 17
Abdul Qasim Hasan Unsari Balkhi, 19
Abdullah Khan Uzbek, 155
Absolute Peace/Universal Peace, xiii, xiv. *See also* Sulh-i kul
Abu Bakr Tusi Haidari, 73
Abul Fazl, xiv, 137, 147, 154, 162–64, 168–70, 172, 174, 178, 182–83
   rise in Mughal court, 167
   theory of state, 162
   as elevation of 'intellect', 163
Ahmad Chap, 68–69, 75, 77, 79–81
Ahmad Mymundi, 22
Ain-i Akbari, 136, 162, 169, 178. *See also* Akbarnama
Aiyar, 22, 27, 29
Ajeet Maal (necklace of invincibility), 8
Akbar, xiii–xiv, 3–4, 111–12, 117–19, 127, 136, 147–84

Chishti Khanqahs (hospices), 160
depression and melancholy, 170
disapproval of gendered social practices, 181–82
fair dispensation of justice, 182–83
Fana, ideas of 161
hunting expedition, 172
Ibadat Khana, 175–78
insistence on Daagh-o Chehra, 177
interest in learning spiritual practices, 161
interest in understanding Hindu beliefs, 166
inter-religious discussions, 176
liberalism, 159
Maktab Khana (translation bureau), 168
open-mindedness, 159
policies towards the Rajputs, 163–70
policy of inclusion, 181
religious tolerance, 192
secular views, 159
Sulh-i kul, 178–84, 188
tendency to experiment, 172

timeline, 149–51
translation of Sanskrit works, 168
vegetarianism, 182
Wahdat ul wujud (unity of existence), 161
Zabaan-i Qudrat, idea of, 172
Akbarnama, xiv, 162, 170–72, 173–175
Akbar And His Age, 148
Alam Khan, 106, 160
Alauddin Khalji
  arrogance and anger, 86
  Ata Juwaini, 160
  bait-and-switch strategy, 76
  betrayal, 99
  economic reforms, 84
  karaamat' (miracles), 85
  'kashf (mystical inspiration), 85
  military skills, 80
  personal bodyguards, 89
  personal inclination, 91
  political expedient policy, 81
  ruthless autocracy of, 68
  stifling rules of, 90
Alauddin Masud Shah, 40, 44
Alauddin Muhammad Shah Khalji Sikandar-i Saani, 68
Al-Biruni, 17
Alexander the Great, 82
Alghu Khan, 81
Ali Quli Khan, 154–55
Almas Beg, 76–77
Alp Khan, 87–88
Amin Khan, 50
Amir Hasan Sijzi, 48

Amir Khusrau, 43, 48, 52, 84, 175, 180
Anderson, Benedict, 193
Antonio Montserrat, 170
Aram Shah, 40–41
Arkali Khan, 68–69, 73, 79–81
Arthashastra, 169
Arz-i-Mamalik (muster master), 55, 64, 87
Askari, 105, 111, 119, 127
Atharva Veda (Atharban), 168
Atka Khan, 171–72
Aurangzeb, 181, 188
  nishan (princely order), 181
Autocratic Mulukiyat, 38

Babur, xiii, 102–5, 108–10, 123–24, 127–28, 133, 148, 157
  Koh-i-Noor, 103
  Chanderi expedition (1528), 133
  excursion to Dholpur, 109
  hectic military career, 110
Badaoni, 4, 161, 164, 166–67, 172, 178
Bahadur Khan Nuhani, 133
Bahlol Lodi, 132
Bahram Shah, 44
Bahubal, King, 7
  Bounty, 4–8
Bairam Beg, 122
Bairam Khan, 118, 152–58, 160
  containment, 152–59
  policy of exclusion, 153
Bajour, battle of (1519), 103
Balban, 45–46, 48, 50–54, 67

Index

principles of strong governance, 53
Bandagaan/ghulaam (slave), 37, 40–41, 53–54, 69, 72, 79, 88
Bastan Nama, 19–22
Bhakti movement, 188
Bhartari, 4, 8–12
Bibi Mahak, 88
Bicultural coinage, 25
Bigeh Begum (Humayun's wife), 128
British Civil Service Commission, 4
Buddhism, 24, 190
Bughra Khan, 51–53, 56–58, 64
Buland Darwaza, 161

'Chabutra-i-Sultani', 65
Chandawar, battle of, 36
Chaugan (medieval polo), 40
Chausa, battle of (1539), 105, 107–8
Chaya Laddha, 161
Chengiz Khan, 39, 41, 102, 160
Christensen, Clayton M., 131
Christian Jesuits, 159
Circle of justice, idea of, 30

Dastur-ul-Afazil, 65
Daulat Khan Lodi, 133
Daulat Shah's, 29
Day of Judgement, 89
De facto ruler. *See* Malik Kafur
Dildar Begum (Babur's wife), 103
Divine Compassion, 179
Divine Right Theory of Kingship, xiii, 46. *See also* Balban
Diwan, 174
Dost Muhammad, 22
Duration-triggered amnesia, x

Elixir of life, 9
European Theory of Social Contract, 162

Faizi, xiv, 161, 168
Fajr azaan (call for the dawn prayers), 142
Fakhruddin Malik ul Umra, 50, 53
Farid Khan. *See* Sher Shah Suri
Fariduddin Ganj-e Shakar, 71
Farman (royal order), 75
Farrukhi, 20–21, 25
Fate, xi, 51
'Fatehnama' (declaration of victory), 81
Fatima Hussain, 48
Fawaid ul Fua'ad, 48
Ferhad Khan, 112
Firdaus, 30
Firdausi, 15, 18–24, 27–30
  betrayal of, xii, 18
  Satire on Sultan Mahmud, 31–34
Fridays congregational prayer, 72, 94
Futuh us-Salatin, 46

Gandharva Sen, 7
'Ganwaars' (local peasants), 135
Gaz-i Sher Shahi, 136
Ghiyasuddin Balban-i Khurd, 46

The Golestan, 101
Gulbadan Begum, 104, 108, 127. See also *Hymayun Nama*
Gulrang and Gulchihra (Babur's daughters), 110
Gung Mahal (palace of the dumb), 172

Haakima (governess) of the harem, 55
Hafiz Shirazi, 174
Haibat Khan, 47
Hamida Banu Begum, 113–15, 155
Harbans Mukhia, xiv, 189–92
Harivansha Purana (*Haribans*), 168
Hasan Nizami, 40
Hazaar Sutun, 89, 93, 98–99
Hind Swaraj, 192
Hindal, 104–5, 109–11, 113–16
How Will You Measure Your Life, 131
Humayun Nama, 104, 113
Humayun, xiii, 101–129, 133–34, 148, 152, 154
   accidental death, 152
   attitude towards life, 129
   childlike enthusiasm, 117
   command over the pen, 123
   feelings for Hamida, 116
   first victory over Afghans, 112
   forgiveness, 123–25
   madness of Love, 113–18
   political compulsions, 111
   war with Sultan Bahadur Shah, 105

Husain Quli Khan, 155
Husamuddin, 92

Ibadat Khana, 166, 175–178
Ibn Batuta, 46
Ibrahim, 72, 80, 98, 102, 123, 132, 168
Ijaz-i-Khusravi, 43
Ikhtiyaruddin Hud, 79
Ikhtiyaruddin Khalji, 66
Imam Ghazai, 177
Imperial army, defeat of, 50
Iqta (Futuh), 71, 74
Iqtadari system, 37
Iqtidar Alam Khan, 158, 160, 162, 174
Iqtidar Husain Siddiqui, xiv, 40–41, 192
Irfan Habib, 134, 144, 148, 162, 169
Ishak Sharif Shah, 20
Ishtiaq Ahmed, 191
Ishtiyaq Ahmad Zillis's, 58
Islamic belief, 24, 72
Islamic ideals, 38
Islamic mysticism, 24
Islamic personal law, 49
Iyar-i Danish, 168

Jahangir, 161, 179–80
   perception of Sulh-i kul, 180–81
Jaharia Barwar, 99
Jai Singh, 188
Jalala Roshani, 163
Jalaluddin Khalji, 64–65, 67–68, 96

Jalaluddin Mangbarni, 41
Jalaluddin Muhammad Akbar. *See* Akbar
Jalaluddin's administration, mildness of, 70
Jamal Khan, 132
Jamal Qiwam, 83
Jamaluddin Yaqut, 43
Jaswant Singh, 188
Jauhar, 119–21, 127
Jawami-al Hikyat wa Lavami-al Rivayat, 40
Jha, D.N., xiv, 192
Jinnah, M.A., 194
Junaid Barlas, 133

Kai Kaus, 66–68, 82
Kaikhusrau, assassination of, 57
'Kalpavriksha', 5
Kamran, 105, 108–9, 111–12, 122, 127
Kannauj, battles of, 36, 105
Karbala, battle of, 38
Karma, theory of, 39
Khalifa of Baghdad, xiii, 23–24, 42
Khalji Revolution, 68
Khan-i Shahid (martyred prince). *See* Prince Muhammad
Khawaja Ghazi Diwan, 124
Khazain-ul Futuh, 43
Khilafat democratic Khilafat, 38
Khilafat, 24
  administrative effectuality of, 38
  legitimacy of, 24

Khirad Afza, 3
Khizr Khan, 86–88, 91, 152
Khurramgah (interim court), 89
Khusrau Khan, 91–93, 95–100
Khwaja Jalaluddin Mahmud, 152
Khwaja Khatir, 54
Khwaja Muazzam, 114, 152
Khwaja Muinuddin Chishti of Ajmer, 160
Khwarizm Shah, 39
Koh-i-Noor, 103, 110
Kṛta, 2

Laila and Majnu, 106
'Lakh-Bakhsh' (endower of lakhs), 39
Lilavati, 168
Lutbaran, 6–7

Mahabharata (Razm-nama), 168
Maham Anga, 154, 156, 183
Maham Begum (Baburs favourite wife), 103
Mahmud Bughra Khan, 50
Mahmud of Ghazni, xii
Mahmud Salim, 78
Mahzar (1579), 177
Majestic paraphernalia, 56
Malik Aitmar Kachchan, 66
Malik Asaduddin, 91
Malik Bahauddin Balban, 44–45
Malik Baq Baq, 47
Malik Chajju, 67, 69
Malik Ikhtiyaruddin Altuniya, 44
Malik Kafur, 87–89
Malik Naib-Wazir, 87

Malik Shahabuddin, 68, 88, 91
Malik Shahak, 55
Malik ul Umra Fakhruddin, 66
Malik Yuzaki, 55
Malika-i Jahan, 79–81
Malikul-Umra Kotwal Fakhruddin, 82
Man Singh, 179. *See also* Akbar
Manichaeism, 24
Mansura, destruction of, 23
Masnavi Dewal Rani Wa-Khizr Khan, 44
Masnawi, 174
Maulana Jalaluddin Rumi, 174
Max Weber, 147
Mehtar Anis, 122
Mir Abdul Latif, xiv, 160
Mir Abul Baqa, 115–16
Mir Musavvir, 22
Mirror of Princes, 169
Mirza Abul Qasim, 154
Mirza Shah Husain, 118
Miyan Hasan, 131
Mohammad Habib, 187
Mongol insurgencies, 48
Montserrat, 163, 174, 179
Mu'azzam Beg, 160
Mubarak Khan, 89
Mubariz Khan Sur (Adil Shah), 152
Mughal polity, 158
Muhammad Awfi, 40
Muhammad Rahim Mirza, 157
Muizzuddin Bahram Shah, 40
Muizzuddin Kaiqubad, 46, 53
Muizzuddin Muhammad Sam, 36, 39

Munim Beg, 152
Munim Khan, 118–19, 153, 155, 160
Muntakhab al Jawahir (Selected Gems), 169
Murad (Akbar's son), 173
Muslim polities, history of, 43
Mutakhab-ut Tawarikh, 35, 167
Myth-making, 16

Nal Daman, 168
Namah-e Khirad Afza, xii, 3
Nasiruddin Mahmud, 40, 44, 48
Nasiruddin Muhammad Humayun. *See* Humayun
National Movement, 193
Nationalism, 187, 191
Natural justice, xiii
Nehru, Jawaharlal, 193–94
Nine sister goddesses, x
Nirgun Bhakti, 179, 188
Nizamuddin Auliya, 43, 48, 83, 86, 89, 94–95, 108, 180
Nizam-ul Mulk Junaidi, 42
Nizamul Mulk Tusi, 177
Non-Sunni Muslims, attacks on, 23
Nurul Haq, 183

Panchatantra, 168
Panipat
  first battle (1526), 102
  second battle (1556), 155
'*Parama-Bhagavata*', 1
Partition of India, 190–91, 194
Persian renaissance, 17

Political incision, 37
Prince Muhammad, 48–52
Prithviraj Chauhan, 36
Prophet Muhammad's ideal of balancing power, 38
The Punjab: Bloodied, Partitioned and Cleansed, 191

Qadr Khan, 68, 79
Qalandar sect (mystic), 50, 73
Qazi Jalaluddin Kashani, 72
Qazi Ziauddin, 96
Qila-i Kuhna mosque, 137
Quran, 45, 77, 108, 177
Qutbuddin Aibak, 39, 41
Qutbuddin Khalji, 68, 90 96
Qutluqh Khan, 45, 48

Rai Kalu, 51
Rai Purushottam, 4
Raja Bhoj, 2, 12
Raja Rana Prasad, 117
Rajputs and Mughals, 163. See also Akbar
Rajtarangini, 168
Ramayana, 168
Ramzaan (Islamic month of fasting), 76
Rana Raj Singh of Mewar, 181
Rationalism, 173
Raushan Beg Kukeh, 124
Raziya, 42–44
Rihla, 46
Ritualism, 173
Roshan Beg, 117
Ruknuddin Firoz, 40, 42–43

Ruknuddin Ibrahim, 68
Rumi Khan, 106
Rustam and Sohrab, tragedy of, 19

Saadi Shirazi, 1, 101
Saiyid Nurul Hasan, 187
Salim, 78, 160–61
Salima Sultan Begum, 3, 157. See also Akbar
Sankh's Sorcery, 4–8
Satish Chandra, xiv, 17, 186
Savarkar, Vir, 194
Secularism, 181, 187, 193
Sedition, 49, 51, 69–70, 75, 82, 96, 133, 158
Shadi Khan, 86, 88, 91, 131
Shah Tahmasp, 22, 105, 124, 126
Shah Turkan, 42–43
Shahnama, xii, 15–16, 18, 22–24, 27–29
  critical role, 16
  hope of being rewarded, 18
  writing style, 16
  See also Firdausi
Shaikh Abdul Haq Muhaddis, 183
Shaikh Abdun Nabi, 175
Shaikh Ahmad Sarhindi, 159, 179
Shaikh Ali, 113, 122
Shaikh Khalil, 138
Shaikh Mubarak, xiv, 161
Shaikhu Baba. See Salim
Shamsuddin Abul Muzaffar Iltutmish, 40
Shamsuddin Kai Kaus, 46
Shayista Khan, 65–66

Sher Khan, 45, 48, 52, 109
Sher Shah Suri, xiii, 105, 107–8, 112, 117, 130–46, 192
  academic proficiency, 132
  balance between rigidity and plasticity, 143
  Chanderi expedition (1528), 133
  Charwadaar, 141
  construction of roads network, 135
  crop rates, 137
  economic reforms, 134
  impact on the administrative system, 134
  implementation of daagh-o-chehra, 136
  man of high-impact resilience, 131
  military trials, 138–39
  observant monarch, 141
  official records, 139–40
  recruitment of a 'nobody', 140–41
  resolution of unanticipated problems, 142–45
  supervised the daagh-o-chehra, 138
  tools of governance, 139–40
  top-down approach, 143
  views on justice, 145–46
  Zabt system of revenue management, 137
Shia Muslims of non-Indian origin, 158
Shireen Moosvi, xiv, 113, 157, 167, 170, 173–74, 192
Sidi Maula, 71
Sikandar Lodi, 136
Sikandar-i Sani (Alexander-II), 82
'Simia' or 'Kimiyasaaz', 71
Singhasan Battisi (*Nama-i Khirad Afza*), xii, 2–3, 11, 168
Siraajul Muluk, 169
Slaves, designation of, 37
Social Contract, Theory of', 147
Somanatha: The Many Voices of a History, 26
State-Society interaction, 189–90
Subhan Quli, 115
Subjective templates, x
Sufi's inclination towards politics, 83
'Sufiyana', 182
Sulh-i kul (Absolute Peace/Universal Peace), xiii–xiv, 147–48, 159, 168, 172–73, 176, 178–184
Sultan Aram Shah, 39–40
Sultan Mohammad, 124
Sultan Qutbuddin Aibak, 39–40
Sultan Ruknuddin Ibrahim, 68, 79
Sultan Shamsuddin Kai Kaus, 46, 65
Sunni Islam, 23, 26
Sunni Muslim nobility, 158
Sunni orthodoxy, 23, 26
  formalism of, 23
'Surah Yasin, 77'. *See also* Quran
Sutun-i Sultanate (pillars of the empire), 42
Syed Athar Abbas Rizvi, 177, 183

Syur-al Muluk/Bastan Nama, 19

Tabaqat-i Nasiri, 40
Tagore, Rabindranath, 191
Tahqiq ma li'l Hind, 17
Tajikanilkanthi, 168
Taj-ul Mathir, 40
Tarain, second battle of, 36
Tardi Beg, 118–19, 152–54
Tarikh-i Akbari, 157
Tarikh-i Fakhr-i Mudabbir, 65
Tarikh-i Firoz Shahi, 51, 58
Tarikh-i-Yamini, 18
Tazkirat-ul-Vaqiyat, 120
Thapar, Romila, 24, 26, 37
Timurid principalities, 160
Tughluqabad, battle of, 153
Tughril Kush, title of, 50
Tuti Namah, 3
Tuzuk-i Jahangiri, 179
Two-nation theory, 191, 194

Ulugh Khan, 45, 68, 81
Unsari, 20–22
Usjudi, 20–21

Valour and Values, 126–29
Vikram Samvat, 1–2, 8
Vikramaditya, xii, 1, 2, 13

Weights and measures, 85

Yak Lakhi Khan, 92
Yaqub Nasir, 85
Yasa-i-Chingezi, 160
Yoghrish Khan, 92

Zafan-i Goya, 65
Zafar Khan, 81, 92
Zahiruddin Muhammad Babur's, 102
Zain al-Akhbar, 25
Zanj people, 23
Ziauddin Barani, 51
Ziauddin Rumi, 94
'Zill-i-Allah', 53
Zoroastrianism, 23–24
Zuhar azaan (call for the afternoon prayer), 142, 144
Zunnnar (Brahmanical thread), 59